HEALING *from* NEGLECT

HEALING *from* NEGLECT

WHEN THOSE WE *Love* DON'T *Love* US

JANENE BAADSGAARD

PLAIN SIGHT
AN IMPRINT OF CEDAR FORT, INC.
SPRINGVILLE, UTAH

ISBN 13: 978-1-4621-1175-6

Published by Plain Sight Publishing, an imprint of Cedar Fort, Inc.
2373 W. 700 S., Springville, UT 84663
Distributed by Cedar Fort, Inc., www.cedarfort.com

LIBRARY OF CONGRESS CATALOGING-IN-PUBLICATION DATA

Baadsgaard, Janene Wolsey, author.
Healing from neglect : when those we love don't love us / by Janene Baadsgaard.
pages cm
Includes bibliographical references and index.
ISBN 978-1-4621-1175-6 (alk. paper)
1. Family violence. 2. Child abuse. I. Title.

HV6626.B22 2013
362.82'92--dc23

2013002991

Cover design by Angela D. Olsen
Cover design © 2013 by Lyle Mortimer
Edited and typeset by Whitney A. Lindsley

Printed in the United States of America

10 9 8 7 6 5 4 3 2 1

For my family

Other books by

JANENE BAADSGAARD

Healing from Abuse
Is There Life After Birth?
A Sense of Wonder
Why Does My Mother's Day Potted Plant Always Die?
On the Roller-Coaster Called Motherhood
Families Who Laugh . . . Last
Grin and Share It: Raising a Family with a Sense of Humor
Sister Bishop's Christmas Miracle
Expecting Joy
Winter's Promise
Fifteen Secrets to a Happy Home
For Every Mother
Family Finances for the Flabbergasted

Contents

Introduction 1

SECTION ONE: RECOGNIZING NEGLECT

1. Defining Neglect 9
2. Describing Neglect 27

SECTION TWO: RESPONDING TO NEGLECT

3. Types of Neglect 47
4. Results of Neglect 61

SECTION THREE: RECOVERING FROM NEGLECT

5. Overcoming Self-Neglect. 87
6. Avenues to Healing. 103

SECTION FOUR: REWRITING NEGLECT

7. The Role of Faith. 127
8. Rewarding Neglect. 141

SECTION FIVE: RELEASING NEGLECT

9. Gifts from Pain 161
10. Discovering Joy 175

About the Author 199

Introduction

Perhaps the greatest joy in life is to love and be loved. The sad truth, however, is that many of us are hurting inside because some of those we choose to love do not love us. We try to cope with the rejection, loss, sadness, or emptiness this reality brings, but the pain doesn't go away. If we have been hurt or disappointed by those we love, especially our parents or partners, it can be difficult to heal and move on. When we try to forget or pretend the heartbreaking relationship doesn't really matter, we discover the hurt is still there. We find ourselves trapped, unable to live an abundant life.

It may be helpful to take a fresh look at our life as though we were authors. Each of us is the main character of our own life story. We are free to choose if we want to be the tragic central character or the hero. We may not be in charge of the plot twists or ill-chosen characters that enter our lives, but we have the power to stand firm at any moment and proclaim, "This is not how my story is going to end."

The problem is we can't write the next chapter of our life if we never stop reliving the last one. We can't expect our life choices to bring different results if we persist in doing what we have been doing. Destructive relationships will continue to hurt us if we don't take the time to understand them, learn something meaningful from our experiences, and choose to heal and move forward. We are not at the mercy of those who choose to abuse and neglect us. We are not trapped in harmful relationships. In fact, looking at all our interactions with fresh eyes will free us to live how we were meant to. The hard fact is this: if we allow those we love to keep making more withdrawals than deposits, the account will eventually be empty. It is wise to know when it is time to close the account.

In every interesting story, unseemly personalities seek to destroy or thwart the mission of the main character. How the protagonist responds determines whether he or she is a courageous or tragic character. One element of a noteworthy story is the difficulties and setbacks the main character must face. If there were no dragon or wicked stepmother, we wouldn't keep reading to see how the story ends. In real life, we all have difficult circumstances and people to deal with. Our mission is to figure out what to do about it so that we will ultimately be the conqueror and not the victim of our own stories.

As a reader, I am particularly frustrated when the main character doesn't appear to recognize his or her adversary. "Don't trust him!" I want to scream just as the protagonist embraces the bad guy. "He wants to hurt you."

The main character, oblivious to the real danger, welcomes the nemesis into his or her life. Thus, the plot thickens and trouble begins. In make-believe stories the enemy is obvious to the reader, but this is not so in real life. The wolf in the forest is more easily detected than the one in Grandmother's nightgown. Often we don't see the impending consequences from remaining in abusive and neglectful relationships when the wolves reside in our own homes.

One reason we fail to recognize our antagonist is that we think we love our abuser and believe that we are the problem. We want to believe that if we are more patient, loving, and forgiving, then the destructive relationship will eventually offer us the opportunity to love and be loved. Sometimes it takes many years before we finally reach a genuine personal awakening or breakthrough. An awakening is the moment when we see our own life in unadulterated reality. A breakthrough is a decisive action we take or a place in time when we find the courage and wisdom to learn from our difficult experiences and the strength and resolve to move on.

One of the best ways to begin a new chapter in life is to understand our past. Awareness of our past will not be useful if we simply want to point fingers, place blame, and feel sorry for ourselves. Understanding our past should give us additional insight into the unconscious reasons for our thoughts, feelings, and behavior today. Looking more closely at a difficult childhood or an unhappy dating or marriage relationship is the way we take back surrendered power, find the motivation to change our response to abuse and neglect, and make steps to move forward with hope. When we fully comprehend the impact of rejection and neglect, we will become a chain-breaker, or the person who stops a painful multigenerational abuse cycle. When we no longer dismiss or minimize the effects of mistreatment in our own lives, we are better able to see reality and make decisions. As the fog lifts, we gradually grow stronger, wiser, and more at peace.

Everyone deserves to be treated with kindness and respect.

Say this out loud three times: *I deserve to be treated with kindness and respect.*

Tragically, we often remain in destructive relationships because that is all we've experienced and we don't know any better. If we've never felt loved, we may not know what it really means to love and be loved. This emptiness makes it more difficult for us to become loving people who choose loving friends and partners. Likewise, if we've never felt safe, it is harder for us to ever truly relax. If we never had enough food or positive attention, it is more difficult for us to feel generous with our resources or our praise. If no one has ever nurtured or cared for us, it follows that we will have a more difficult time knowing how to nurture and care for ourselves. Even though it may be more difficult, each of us can become a person who knows how to love and be loved. A loving person is not a pretend character in a fairy tale. A loving person is real. True love really is the only thing that lasts.

Belief comes first. We have to believe it is possible to live a life where we love and are loved. Imagination comes next. We have to imagine a better life than the one we know. Everything is created in our minds before it becomes real. Becoming a loving person able to offer and receive true love is a real option. Our life stories have a possible happy ending.

Now is the time to stop hiding, minimizing, or justifying our destructive relationships. We can stop the day-to-day struggle, the going from crisis to crisis, and the constant soul battering by the destructive relationship in our lives. We always have a choice. We can stop the drama and trust the goodness in life and in ourselves. We can expect better from our relationships. This is the moment to choose a more meaningful way to live and love—a better way to care for ourselves and those around us.

Listen very carefully . . . *everyone deserves to be cared for and loved . . . including you.*

To begin, *you* must be the person who loves and cares about you now.

NOTE: Sometimes I have referred to both the person who abuses and neglects and the victim as "he or she," while at other times, I have chosen one or the other. I don't mean to imply that a person who abuses and neglects should be viewed as primarily male or the victim as primarily female—or vice versa. Both are all too commonly found in both genders.

Also, we all participate in relationships that shape our identity. Mothers, fathers, siblings, grandparents, dating partners, spouses, teachers, coaches, church leaders, and children are some of the important relationships that most affect us. For simplicity's sake, in this book I have primarily referred to the abuser in destructive and neglectful relationships as a partner or parent.

Section One
Recognizing Neglect

Chapter One

DEFINING NEGLECT

Descriptions for abuse and neglect are often paired in clinical definitions because most of the time they occur together. Yet neglect often gets second billing because it isn't considered as devastating by those who are uninformed. Obvious abuse makes the headlines. Unseen neglect is seldom reported or understood. The wicked witch in *Hansel and Gretel* seems scarier than the mother and father who take their children out into the forest and leave them there. Yet all of these characters hurt children. As a result, those who have been neglected are often left alone to sort out their confusing feelings and subsequent behavior. In fact, neglect may be the most difficult wound to heal.

Few people start out intending to harm those they might have loved, yet many do. Whether this harm is intentional or not, those who have been neglected need gentle assistance to understand what has happened to them. Those who have survived rejection need new ideas and models for how to think and live differently in the present. They need to know how to form healthy relationships and the steps necessary to heal if they don't want to hand this heartbreak to their children.

Many of us unknowingly select a partner who is much like one of our parents. If we have been abused or neglected, we often marry someone who continues to abuse and neglect us;

or we become the person who abuses or neglects our partner because it feels normal. When children arrive, we often feel like children ourselves, struggling with our own personal, financial, and marital challenges. As a result, most of us default to parenting the same way we were parented. Even though we said we'd never treat our children the way we were treated, we often do. Then we feel guilty and chalk up our failure as one more proof our inner negative labels are true. We believe we really are failures. Listen very carefully . . . *no one is a failure.*

Once we understand abuse and neglect, we can finally let go of the brainwashing we received. This mind manipulation told us that we are not worthy of love, that we'll never be good enough, and that our mistakes make us bad people. The truth is—we are all worthy of love, we are all good enough, and our mistakes do not make us bad people.

Rejection and neglect are common. We have all been neglected in some way, and we have all neglected someone—most likely ourselves. It takes courage to face this reality and then make the decision to change the only people we have any control over . . . us. We don't have to repeat the same behavior as our parents. We are not predestined to become the uncaring partner we have experienced. We are not trapped in familial patterns that perpetuate patterns of mistreatment. In fact, if we choose to educate and enlighten ourselves, we can develop the new heart and the proficiencies we need to turn this empty, negative way of living around forever. When those we love don't love us back, it doesn't mean we are inadequate or unlovable; it simply means that those loved ones are not capable of loving us right now.

CHILD NEGLECT

Child neglect, by definition, is a passive form of abuse where the parents or caregivers do not provide an environment or experiences that promote emotional stability, a sense of protection, and an atmosphere where children feel loved, wanted, and safe. Neglect is a form of soul violence that injures the mind, heart, and humanity of a child. Neglect has been associated with the failure of the brain to form properly and can lead to impaired mental, physical, and emotional development. To classify as neglect, the behavior of the caregiver must not be the result of poverty, cultural norms, or lack of education.

If a child's ability to form attachments with her caregivers is disrupted early in life, the child will have difficulty forming healthy relationships throughout her life. The first few years are vital. Sensitive periods for development occur in those early years. Neural synapses are formed at high rate. After the first few years, these synapses begin to be pruned according to their use. Certain pathways that are left unused are eventually discarded, and opportunities for the child's development are lost.

Physical neglect is the failure to provide the goods, services, and time necessary to encourage the normal growth and development of those who can't provide those needs for themselves. Basic needs are food, shelter, clean water, a safe environment, educational opportunities, personal hygiene facilities, adequate supervision, and prompt medical care.

Abandonment is the most common cause of physical neglect. According to the US Census Bureau, half of American children are growing up without their biological father. Abandonment is defined as desertion of a child and/or failure to take responsibility for their needs. Expelling a child from the home before the child is old enough to deal with the realities of independent living is another form of neglect. Constantly shuttling a child around for days, weeks, or months into the care of others also classifies as neglect.

Neglected children may be fed but lack a nutritional diet. Neglected children may be clothed but lack clothing that is clean or appropriate for their size or the season. Neglected children are often left unattended at home or in a car. Neglected children are exposed to safety and sanitary hazards such as cigarette smoke and unsanitary household conditions like rotting food or human or animal feces.

Failure to show normal healthy physical affection through loving touch is another form of neglect. Parents also neglect children when they choose inappropriate caregivers. Neglect is the failure to protect children by leaving them in the care of someone who should not be trusted to provide care. For example, known abusers or those with a substance addiction should never be allowed to care for children.

Corrupting is a form of neglect where the parent provides an environment where alcohol, drugs, or other harmful items like guns and pornography are readily available. Involving a child in illegal activities such as shoplifting and sexual activities is also a form of abuse and neglect referred to as corrupting. When parents throw children out of the home before they are equipped to provide for themselves, the children are left at the mercy of those who will further corrupt them. Some parents neglect their children because they have not healed from their own past abuse. For example women who have been sexually abused are three times more likely to neglect their children.

Emotional neglect includes the failure to love, nurture, provide positive support, guidance, acknowledgment, and affection. Neglectful parents show scant interest in the child's thoughts, feelings, activities, and problems. They do not see their children as vulnerable, innocent, and precious; they see their children as burdens, objects to manipulate, or servants who are obligated to take care of the parent. Neglectful parents force their children to assume adult roles and make them a dumping ground for marital issues. Conversations are calculated to hurt, control, intimidate, punish, belittle, or harm. Rejection and neglect are accomplished with harsh tone of voice, threats, vulgarity, intimidation, sulking, tirades, angry outbursts, lack of interest, abandonment, and extramarital affairs.

Educational neglect is the failure of the caregiver to provide an environment where effective learning can take place. To be able to learn, a child's brain needs to be in a state of attentive calm. Constant drama, chaos, abuse, and neglect in the home forces a child's brain to become hypervigilant. When a child lives in anxiety and fear, he can't focus on learning. Neglectful parents often require that the child take on parental responsibilities to the neglect of homework or extracurricular activities. Permitting chronic truancy is also a form of educational neglect.

Psychological neglect is perhaps the most common and detrimental form of abuse inflicted on children. It is a conscious and repeated effort to destroy a child's peace of mind, security, or self-confidence. This is accomplished in subtle ways such as deliberately frightening a child and encouraging a child to remain dependent or feel responsible for the parents' well-being. Neglectful parents do not allow their child to have close friends, develop talents, or pursue interests. As a result, the child becomes dependent on the parent.

At the other extreme, neglectful parents will pick their children's friends, decide what talents the children must pursue, and put pressure on them to overachieve. This type of neglectful parent tries endlessly to amass reflected glory through his or her child's achievements. Neglectful parents put pressure on their children to constantly add to their list of accomplishments in order to finally receive the elusive parental approval that never comes. What these parents neglect is the reality of their children's unique and irreplaceable soul. These parents do not understand that their children are separate human beings with magnificent lives to experience, personal choices to make, and the God-given freedom to become who they choose to be.

Perhaps the most traumatizing experience for a child is the absence of love, affection, or any form of mature, selfless emotional giving from a parent. This kind of neglect is often connected to a role reversal in which the child is required to become a living antidepressant for the parent, endlessly attempting to fill the narcissistic parent's emotional void. Eventually the parent and child don't know how to separate and lead different, mature, and fulfilling lives. The parent clings to the child like a person who is drowning, and the child can't detach without feeling like they are abandoning the parent.

In reality, the parent has abandoned the responsibility to grow up and become an unselfish and self-sustaining adult, and has instead chosen to bind the child to himself in mentally and emotionally unhealthy ways. This sick relationship will eventually destroy the adult child's chances for happiness with a present or future partner and children. Selfish or narcissistic people are not really interested in close relationships. They are inwardly repulsed by emotional closeness. Yet they are so self-absorbed that they refuse to let go of those they use, abuse, neglect, and manipulate.

Psychological neglect is also accomplished with cruel mental games of control and degradation that deny the child any sense of emotional security. The effects of terrorizing, belittling, or neglecting a child are just as traumatic as any other form of abuse. Making it impossible for a child to protect herself, negative brainwashing, forced isolation, and encouraged illness are other forms of psychological neglect.

Childhood neglect of any type is especially damaging because children do not have the power to leave their harmful relationships. Those who have been neglected while they are young have experienced significant trauma that should never be minimized or ignored. Anything that causes a child to feel helpless or interferes with his ability to feel safe, secure, and loved impedes normal development into adulthood. For example, neglected children often don't trust others and have a difficult time understanding other's emotions. They have a limited ability to feel remorse or empathy and often hurt others without feeling their actions are wrong. Those who are neglected often demonstrate a lack of confidence and social skills. Many neglected children don't know how to resolve their anger and have a difficult time achieving mature independence and empowerment. Childhood neglect is perhaps the most confusing form of abuse because it leaves victims bewildered about what happened to them, mixed up about how to respond, and ill-informed about how to overcome the lasting effects.

One woman described the neglect in her childhood home this way:

> When I was growing up, I was required to be the mother. When I came home from school, I could tell when my twin sisters had been left all day in their cribs by the smell that hit me when I walked through the door. Bored from being left alone for so long, my baby sisters would resort to smearing the contents of their diapers all over themselves, their blankets, mattress, and walls. As soon as she heard me walk through the door, my mother would tell me to clean up the mess. It wasn't until I was a mother with my own children that I realized my baby sisters had been neglected. I didn't know enough about neglect back then to report what was happening in my home. I didn't even realize that I was also neglected. I thought everyone had a mother who stayed in bed all day or all month whenever she felt like it."

One of the reasons neglected children don't receive the intervention they need is that they don't know they are being neglected. A child only knows what he has experienced and believes that what goes on in his home goes on in all homes. To compound the problem, any attempt the child makes to complain about what is going on is dismissed, ignored, or worse, used as an excuse to threaten or abuse the child. So children do not even know they have been manipulated into secrecy. That is why it is so important for other adults in the schools, churches, or communities to notice subtle signs of neglect and make attempts to rescue the child.

Children's minds and hearts need tender, loving, and consistent care to grow and develop as a physically, mentally, spiritually, and emotionally healthy people. Children are incredibly vulnerable. They have no way to know that they need their perceptions validated and their uniqueness respected. Children rely on their caregivers to help them form a compassionate view of themselves. Children are just beginning to learn how they fit into the world. They need the opportunity to see themselves as people who deserve a safe place to live and the right to express themselves. Children need to know they have the power to affect and participate in what happens to them. Instead, neglected children have no control. They feel chronically helpless, ashamed, angry, terrified, guilty, and scared.

One boy in foster care said,

> My mom had lots of boyfriends. They were mean to me. They touched my private parts. Sometimes Mom would leave with her boyfriends for a long time. I took care of myself. I ate noodles dry out of the package. I slept on a dirty mattress in a basement with no heat. I was cold. Mom brought me candy when she came back. I was happy to see her. My aunt told [on her] and some people came and got me and put me in another family. They didn't like me and sent me to another family. My mom didn't do what the judge said she had to do. She didn't want me back. I must be bad and that's why she doesn't want me.

Parents are mirrors for their children; the child literally sees himself the way the parent sees him. This is one reason why neglect leaves such deep wounds. Adult survivors who were abused and neglected as children really don't know how wonderful they are. They are confused about their worth. In an effort to ease their pain, they often increase it by blaming themselves for how they are treated. Or they get stuck in anger and bitterness and stay angry and bitter for the rest of their lives. Adult survivors of neglect are often confused about why they continue to struggle with trust issues, anxiety, low self-esteem, depression, addictions, anger, destructive relationships, health issues, and an inability to establish safe personal boundaries.

Children always blame themselves when they are not safe or loved because it gives them the illusion that they have some control in their life. It is almost impossible for children to see their parents or caregivers as they really are. Facing the reality that your parent does not love you and is not there for you is simply too much to bear and would overwhelm their psyche. Facing this reality is so difficult that many adults who were not loved by their parents or caregivers never choose to feel that pain. Instead they remain in denial, crippling their ability to love their own partner and children.

SIGNS OF CHILD ABUSE AND NEGLECT

As a society and as individuals we need to stand taller and declare, "No more" and mean it. We need to take action when we become aware of the abuse or neglect of children in our circle of influence. We can no longer tolerate destructive behavior at any level without fully comprehending that we are part of the problem.

When children are being abused and neglected, the signs are sometimes subtle and confusing. The following symptoms are red flags that should get our attention:

- Overreaction to physical contact
- Overly frightened of and submissive to parents or other authority figures
- Substance abuse
- Allows extreme father or mother dominance

- Isolation from community
- Role reversal between parent and child
- Immature behavior
- Inability to make friends
- Wearing clothes that are dirty and not appropriate for current seasonal conditions
- Low achievement or obsessive high achievement
- Constant fearfulness
- Accident-prone
- Cheating, stealing, or lying
- Destructiveness to self and others
- Aggressive behavior
- Withdrawal
- Overcompliance to the demands of others
- Always hungry
- Listless and tired
- Always caring for younger siblings
- Poor hygiene
- Decaying teeth
- Infected sores

Infants do not have the ability to tell us in words that something is wrong; but their bodies, expressions, and development delays are red flags to watch for. A newborn that is addicted to drugs is an obvious victim of abuse and neglect. Failure to thrive in babies is less obvious and equates to poor muscle tone, unhappy facial expressions, few vocalizations, and general unresponsiveness.

Behaviors to watch for in adults that might indicate neglectful parenting include:

- Indifference to the child
- Depressed attitude
- Irrational behavior
- Drug or alcohol addiction
- Blames child for problems
- See child as worthless, burdensome, and bad
- Look to child for care of emotional needs

ADULT NEGLECT

Neglect in adult relationships is the conscious and repeated failure to provide the goods, services, time, or attention to meet your partner's physical, spiritual, emotional, intellectual, and social needs. Adults who neglect their spouses do not provide experiences that promote stability, a sense of protection, feelings of being loved, or an environment where the spouse feels safe and secure.

Physical neglect in a marriage relationship is the unwillingness to provide the necessities of life such as food, clothing, and shelter. This failure to provide can be a result of many things including substance abuse, addictions, mental illness, or long-term unemployment. Failure to provide is sometimes a result of a partner's inability to keep employment because of behavioral issues. Physical neglect is also the failure to provide physical affection by loving touch and sexual intimacy.

Emotional neglect is the failure to spend time with and give attention to your partner. This behavior can range from simply ignoring a spouse because you think you are too busy to vindictively withholding love, affection, and communication as a form of punishment. All behavior that persistently destroys self-confidence and emotional security in your spouse is also a form of neglect. Making major decisions without consulting your partner, controlling all finances, and engaging in frequent and separate recreational activities that don't involve the partner is also a form of neglect.

Neglect is one of the major causes of divorce. Both men and women can be neglected in a marriage. Many dating partners who were attentive and affectionate during the courtship period gradually find less and less time and loving concern for their spouse after marriage. Careers, sports, recreation, friends, computer activities, children, in-laws, social affairs, community, or church service now take precedence over their primary relationship with their spouses.

The following are common responses of neglected partners:

- "I feel bad all the time because I feel alone and abandoned."
- "We used to be friends. We aren't anymore."
- "The only time he pays attention to me is when he wants sex."
- "She is never there when I need her the most."

One woman described the loneliness in her marriage this way:

> My husband was so warm and talkative before we were married. He couldn't spend enough time with me. Then after we married and life got more and more stressful, he just quit talking to me or spending time with me. I know he has a lot of pressure at work and in his church work. But he comes home late every night. He doesn't have time for me. I feel like we're roommates. When I try to talk to him about it, he just shuts down and tells me I'm criticizing him. I don't know what to do.

Adults who neglect their family were often neglected themselves as children, or they are following a pattern their parents modeled for them. Often we don't realize there is a better way to live. Unhealed adults of childhood neglect have not felt their pain or done the difficult work of healing.

One man described the loneliness in his marriage this way:

> My wife was so into me before we got married. After the kids came, she acted like I didn't exist anymore. She never wants to be intimate. I've been turned down so many times I don't even want to try anymore. She spends all her time, attention and affection on the children. All she wants from me is a paycheck. I feel angry and confused. I lie in bed feeling alone and empty every night.

When we don't have positive, loving relationships in our homes, we all suffer. Husbands and wives should not make major decisions until they have an enthusiastic agreement between both partners. When we shut our partners out of our careers, finances, recreation, childcare, or religious service, we neglect their need to feel important to us and live with us as an equal partner.

Even if we have not yet experienced a loving partnership, we can work toward creating one. We are not doomed to repeat what we have experienced. In fact, understanding the consequences of abuse and neglect gives us an opportunity to stop this tragedy. We can change our lives and the lives of our posterity if we choose to understand destructive relationships, heal, and create homes where each member of the family is valued. When multigenerational abuse and neglect are no longer part of our family dynamic, a new generation has the opportunity to be raised with the love and nurture necessary to live a full and meaningful life.

Asking the Big Questions

When a child or partner is neglected, his shiny soul gets turned off, buried, forgotten, or lost. Like a flower without adequate water or sunshine, the child or partner's ability to grow, blossom, and produce good fruit becomes limited by the gardener's lack of attention and care. I believe children and partners who are neglected can choose to replant their hearts in loving relationships where they are safe and loved. Then they can create an environment where their individuality can be set free. Hearts that were once neglected can blossom again.

All of us ask the following questions from those closest to us.

- "Do you love me?"
- "Are you there for me?"
- "Do you care about me?"
- "Can I count on you?"
- "Can you put my needs ahead of yours?"

When the answer to those questions is yes, we can relax; we have the opportunity to grow and develop without barriers. If the answer is no, we are held back for a season with many obstructions to normal healthy development.

Often we don't want to see the troubled parent, child, or neglectful partner. Why? We have been told so often that we are the problem that we believe the lie. Or we love our abuser and don't want to get him in trouble. We need to understand that our abuser is already in trouble. When we hold him accountable for his actions we open the possibility of change and healing for both of us.

When we are being abused and neglected, we are not mentally and emotionally healthy enough to see our life with any sense of reality. We live in a fog. Our perspective of our abuser is confused and conflicted. Our perspective of reality is unclear and distorted. Our perception of self is a negative collection of lies from our abuser. We are quite simply confused about who we are and what we need to do.

Abusers are expert at feeding self-doubt by insisting their victims are the problem. They believe that those they abuse cause their behavior. Abusers deny accountability for their words and actions or inactions, apologize without sincerity, or refuse to feel true remorse for the pain they cause others. Those who abuse have developed a habit of dealing with the stresses and difficulties of life by blaming others and taking it out on those around them. They project their fears, failures, insecurities, and jealousies onto others and accuse those closest to them of character flaws they refuse to see in themselves.

Many abusers have not healed from the wounds of their past. They are living with repressed, unhealed pain. Until they can feel their own pain, abusers deny or dismiss the pain they cause others. Abusers continue to be the source of pain in others until they take sole responsibility for their behavior and then change their behavior. One woman told me about her destructive marriage and eventual decision to end the verbal and emotional abuse she endured.

> Two days ago, I left my counselors office and went to a bookstore, in hopes of finding a book that could help bring me comfort. I have been searching bookstores for more than twenty years, hoping to find a book on verbal and emotional abuse. For thirty-six years, I have known that things were not right, but the only sources I could find in my church discussed not being so selfish and trying harder to make my spouse happier. Because of those books and articles, I essentially gave away every right to love and respect, let him do whatever he wanted, never voiced an opinion, and was convinced that I was the problem.
>
> He grasped upon this newfound sense of control and raged forward to crush my spirit while trying to raise his own sense of self-worth. As I lay curled up on a bed in fetal position last December, after an hour of being yelled at, accused, condemned, told that I was the cause of all that was wrong, I prayed throughout the whole night for the Lord to take me home. As it continued the next day, the [Lord's] Spirit came upon me in a feeling of warmth and peace. I knew that the time to leave had come. However, even in doing so, I have been plagued with a sense of failure and wondering if I will ultimately be condemned for leaving a marriage. Was I giving away every blessing and chance that I had for going to heaven by filing for a divorce? Maybe I

was really a sick person and did not know it! Was I just not willing to look at what a horrible person I had become? Could it be that I was in denial, and not my husband? Was I the problem?

My husband affirmed the answer to these questions was, "Yes."

My counselor began to help me see what was really happening at home, and that the answer to these questions was actually a resounding, 'No!' I began to feel that I was doing the right thing by leaving, in spite of my grown children's protests. I gained strength and confidence. But the questions about the eternal consequences I might face continued to plague me. For weeks I had prayed to have some answers. . . . I prayed that there might be a book to help me and answer my questions, so that I could feel the peace I so desperately wanted. The next day, I went to the bookstore and felt prompted to buy your book *Healing from Abuse*. Thank you so much! Your descriptions of the abuser and the abused describe so perfectly the life that I have led for thirty-six years. The scriptures and quotes, along with the explanations and interpretations of their meaning have helped to give me a sense of peace and purpose that I have never possessed. Realizing that by leaving, I am stopping the abuse and am actually helping him to not further condemn himself is a huge help. Thank you so much. My only wish is that your book had been available thirty years ago, when I searching for such answers back then! I am finally beginning to look forward to the rest of my life."

When we are mentally well, we choose to love and care for people who treat us with respect and kindness. We make a mentally healthy decision to love those who are capable of loving us in return. Children, on the other hand, have no choice; they are trapped in their family situation. They can't remove themselves from unhealthy relationships. Because they get accustomed to being treated in destructive ways, eventually their mental health suffers.

When we are not mentally healthy, we continue to choose or remain in relationships throughout life that repeat the abusive or neglectful ones we experienced as children. This may be an unconscious attempt to fix the relationship issues we experienced in the past. In truth, mentally and emotionally unhealthy people are not going to be able to maintain a healthy relationship with each other. Imagine Cinderella staying with her stepmother and hoping things would get better for her entire life. That would be such a depressing story, and we all know how that plot would turn out. We just need to face the facts. If we keep choosing people to love who can't love us back—we are mentally stuck. But we can get unstuck.

Even though we often yearn for someone to love us completely, we should understand that most of us are just practicing. We are emotionally needy people who want to be loved before we offer love. Instead of searching for affection and tenderness in all the wrong people, we can choose to be an eager student in the art of love. Then we can choose to love those who are also willing pupils. Those who abuse and neglect us are not capable of loving us at this point in their moral or ethical progression. Instead of continually going back to a destructive relationship, we must make a choice. If we choose to do nothing, we choose to continue being abused and neglected. The choice we make affects not only us but also our abuser and future generations.

If we choose to leave a destructive relationship, we will discover there are many mentally and emotionally healthy people out there willing to practice the art of love with us. When we walk away from all the cruel drama and the people who create it, we discover it is possible to keep someone in our hearts but not in our lives. Life is too short to waste precious years trying to convince people that they are harming us when they live in a different reality. Decisions must be made. We need a zero tolerance policy for abuse and neglect in our hearts, homes, communities, and nations.

A full and rich life is the result of practicing the art of love. Too often we postpone ending a destructive relationship because we love our abuser. There is a greater way to love. The most caring action we can take is to draw a line in the sand. Tolerating abuse and neglect is not an act of love or virtue. When we truly love our abusers, we understand that holding them accountable for their actions is the highest form of love: a compassionate response that requires courage.

Far too many of us have spent much of our lives figuratively asleep much like the royal court in Sleeping Beauty's castle. We passively accept the circumstances and relationships in our lives and postpone taking any definitive action. It is time to wake up. There is a reason why love's first kiss had the power to wake the napping princess. Loving and being loved is what it means to create an authentic life; the rest is just sleepwalking. Because we are the authors of our own lives, we can change the plot of our story at any moment in time. We can act instead of being acted upon. We can honor the precious and fleeting life we have been given. In reality, only true love can transform a house of selfish, needy, egotistical, self-absorbed people into a warm, vibrant, caring, and joyful family.

We begin with the hope that a loving family is possible. Then we choose to be that transforming golden seed that will later become our eventual harvest. All love begins with us. We choose to learn and grow in the art of love until we become a truly loving person. A Sleeping Beauty or a courageous prince resides deep within all of us. There is a way to have a happy ending to our story.

Chapter Two

DESCRIBING NEGLECT

Types and levels of negligence cover a wide spectrum. Cinderella's stepmother ignored her needs and forced her to do all the chores, while the queen in Snow White tried to poison her. When we neglect those who are dependent on us for nurture and love, we set in motion a chain of damaging events and destructive relationships that harm an ever-widening circle. In real life, no prince is there to come to our rescue. We must stop the abuse and neglect and rescue ourselves.

We seldom think of neglect as abuse. Instead we feel defective or embarrassed if we have been ignored, rejected, or abandoned. We keep the awful secret by absorbing the shame and guilt the abuser refuses to feel. Often we continue the neglect as we ignore, reject, or abandon our own painful feelings. Buried feelings never die; they follow us around wherever we go. There is no escape by avoidance. The only way to find peace is to feel the pain we'd rather avoid. Something beautiful and meaningful is waiting for us when we stop avoiding pain and have the courage to experience it.

One woman spoke of the neglect in her life this way:

> My husband and I used to visit our parents on Sunday evenings. We alternated each week. For years my mother would

> lock herself in her bedroom when we came over. It hurt but I never said or did anything about it because I was accustomed to my parents treating me in confusing and hurtful ways. Then one day my father told me not to come over to their home any more unless he called and invited us. I waited and waited and waited. He never called. I never talked about this situation to anyone because I was embarrassed that my own parents didn't want to see me or my children. I just kept waiting for the phone call that never came and felt devastated. Then I found out that my dad was telling people I was a horrible daughter because I didn't come over to see them.

Why We Don't Leave

Being neglected is every bit as confusing and traumatizing as being abused. Is it worse to be beaten daily or never to hear the words "I love you"? Is it worse to be molested or have your father or husband walk out the door and never come back? Certainly there is no better or worse, for all forms of abuse and neglect cause great pain and leave deep scars. We can't minimize, deny, or pretend away destructive relationships. We have to deal with them head on. Now that we know better, we can do better. The rules have changed from don't feel, don't talk, and don't stop abuse and neglect to talk, feel, and stop abuse and neglect.

We can't create a healthy loving world, nation, or community if we don't create loving homes. We can't be indifferent any longer; the time has come to stop silently submitting to cruel behavior. There is no healing without safety. There is no safety without peace. There is no peace without courage. Where there is great courage, there is great love. It is an act of love to put an end to cruelty, to speak up, respond differently, and stop neglect. It is an act of love to hold those who abuse accountable for their behavior. No one is trapped in a relationship; there is an escape. Love can redeem every suffering. Love is the miracle medicine and the cure. When we truly love someone we hold him accountable for his behavior every time.

Too often we remain in destructive relationships because on some level we don't want to feel the pain of being unloved. Acknowledging painful emotions is difficult for victims because we have had lots of practice trying not to feel what we feel. We get so good at numbing our thoughts or practicing underreactions that pretty soon we really don't know how we feel. This unacknowledged or subconscious pain affects both our physical, emotional, mental, and spiritual health. It hurts when we love someone and he doesn't love us back, but we can recover from that pain. We can't recover from that hurt if we continue to deny, dissociate, repress, or live in a fantasy.

The ability to feel personal anguish can be a great liberator and a loving teacher. Emotional pain is our subconscious trying to get our attention. When we actually experience our own hidden pain, it metaphorically breaks our heart so that we can face reality. Only after we experience our raw personal anguish can we move forward in emotional maturity. Those who are mature are able to see how they are harming others and how others are harming them. We must see reality before we can choose a better way. When we are emotional healthy, we can begin practicing the art of loving and being loved.

Neglect has the power to influence everything in our lives—how we view ourselves and others, the spouse we choose, the career we pursue, the clothes we wear, how we treat our children, how we deal with stress, and our ability to be affectionate. The list goes on and on. If we don't realize we were neglected or mistreated and what that experience has done to us, we can't heal from the damage. We are also more likely to pass along our unhealed pain to the next generation. Though we can't change the past, we can most certainly learn from it.

Looking for Clues from Our Past

Like an archaeologist has to dig through a lot of dirt before the treasure is found, it is often interesting or insightful to dig through our past in an effort to find possible reasons for our present thoughts and behavior. If we were neglected or mistreated as children, we may have been changed in ways we don't now realize or understand. A real possibility also exists that we may have been neglected in the years before we have conscious memory.

The most confusing form of neglect occurs when the people who neglect us claim their actions are for a higher good . . . and we believe those claims. Examples of this type of neglect include the workaholic parent or spouse who unnecessarily works day and night or the parent or spouse who constantly leaves child or partner unattended while performing church or community service. No one has adequate excuses or reasons to neglect those who are dependent on their love and concern. One woman shared her confusing family story with me.

> My mother used to work on genealogy obsessively. She left me alone to tend my siblings day after day. If I ever said anything about her absence, she yelled at me or gave me a long lecture about the importance of doing your family history work. I don't think it occurred to her that she was creating *our* family history and it was becoming one of abandonment and neglect. Even when my teenage unmarried sister got pregnant, she didn't change her habits. Because I was married at the time, I was expected to adopt my nephew and take care of him. So I did. My mother still continues to leave and not tell anyone where she is going for days or weeks. My parents eventually divorced, but they remarried. The extended family is a mess, and I have problems with anxiety and depression. I'm in counseling and just beginning to learn how to set healthy boundaries. My mother still controls the family by telling us what awful children we are. She stops communicating with me if I don't do what she tells me to do. I still struggle with how much contact to have

with my extended family. I can tell my friends to get away from toxic people, but I have a hard time doing it myself.

One of the ways to change a family pattern of abuse and neglect is to take the time to remember and think about our childhood. For an adult who was abused or neglected as a child, remembering the past will seem scary at first. Yet only by remembering can we uncover our original pain and take an objective and mature look at it.

Many of us become adults with a vague idea that our childhood was not particularly happy, but we can't really put our finger on what happened. We decide our experience was pretty typical because we have no idea what a healthy childhood looks or feels like. The way our parents, caregivers, or partners speak to us has become our inner voice. Sometimes, when we are trying to fall asleep or when we are dealing with people who have personalities similar to our neglectful parents or spouses, memories, or flashbacks of past, experiences will come back to haunt us. Most of the time, we push these memories and feelings away. Sometimes we try to keep busy so we don't have to think or remember. We find ways to numb out. No matter what we do, buried memories and feelings return. When they do, we're not even sure how we feel about them because by now we are experts at denying our emotions. The time has come to get those negative, fearful and toxic thoughts out of our head. One way to do that is to remove the toxic people from our life.

Sometimes it helps to give words to what we may have experienced. Perhaps these are some of these memories that will come to mind as you review your past:

- being given up for adoption
- being left alone for a long time in our crib, playpen, or at the hospital
- being pushed aside for another sibling

- looking into your parents' eyes and seeing emptiness
- listening to your parents fight day after day
- going to court for a divorce
- being forgotten at Christmas time or on your birthdays
- never having your parents around
- being the victim of violent anger
- being left to take care of yourself or your siblings at a young age
- feeling hungry and not having enough food to eat
- looking for someone in the crowd at your school activities who never came
- wearing dirty clothes that didn't fit
- losing a loved one at a tender age without anyone to help you deal with the loss
- dealing with maturation without anyone to explain what was happening to your body
- not being taken to the doctor when you had a major injury or illness
- crying in your bed at night because of a night time abuser who hurt you
- hiding in the basement
- taking care of your parents because of an addiction
- never inviting your friends to your home because you were ashamed of your living conditions
- long-term reliance on government/church assistance
- being left home alone with your siblings for long periods
- being placed in foster care
- being forced to sleep in a bed you had urinated in
- dealing with a mouth full of cavities from lack of proper dental hygiene

- bouncing from one foster family to another
- longing for someone to protect you from a violent parent
- wondering if your parents will be there when you wake up
- "walking on egg shells" for fear of angering a family member
- having sores in private places because of lack of training in personal hygiene
- coming home to an empty house over and over again
- feeling sad, scared, or belittled with no one to comfort you
- finding out that your parent lied to you
- being misunderstood and harshly punished
- feeling ignored at a vulnerable time
- being shamed, yelled at, or threatened when you expressed your feelings or opinion
- having one parent hurt you while the other parent stood by and watched
- being told you were ugly, stupid, awkward, dumb, clumsy, or worthless
- feeling responsible for a parent's addiction
- being taught to hate one gender
- being encouraged or forced to perform criminal or immoral acts
- being encouraged or forced to try addictive substances
- being taught that the world is an evil and scary place

Destructive Patterns

Remembering is only a part of the puzzle. After remembering our past, it helps to look objectively at our present behavior to see if we are still caught in a destructive pattern. For example: we were neglected, so now we neglect ourselves; we were ignored and mistreated, so now we ignore and mistreat ourselves; we were not loved, so now you don't know how to love; we were abandoned, so now we are overly clingy with our spouse and children; we weren't loved, so now we continue to form relationships with people who do not love us. On the other hand, it may be that we were neglected, so now we neglect our children. We were ignored, so now we ignore our spouse or children. Either way, we are not living the life we were meant to live. We can change all that now.

Another destructive pattern many adults who were neglected as children exhibit is the constant internal fear that something bad is going to happen. This pattern of thinking was learned in childhood when something bad usually did happen. Without a caring adult to help us deal with all the distressing things that happen to us as children, we grow up with overwhelming and irrational fear. If we always have to face every challenge on our own, life is just too much to navigate successfully. We have an overabundance of adrenaline in our system and must stay on hyper alert. We can't relax, because we never know what bad thing is going to happen next. We never feel safe.

One man told me about the day when he finally allowed himself to feel the deep sorrow he'd carried since he was a small child:

> My father left me and my mother when I was a little boy. I blamed myself. I thought if I wasn't a bad boy, he wouldn't have left. I was constantly afraid my mother would leave me too. We struggled financially. After I grew up, I had anger issues. I was always popping off at the people at work or my wife and children at home over stupid stuff. I didn't understand my flash anger

> any better than anybody else. Outside, I blamed everybody else. Inside, I hated myself. I knew I'd never be good enough. Some days it was everything I could do to get out of bed. I couldn't tell my wife how I felt because I was afraid she'd leave me too. One day I really couldn't get out of bed. My wife found me curled up under the covers. All the awful things that happened to me as a kid exploded inside me. When I remembered, it is absolute terror. My wife walked in the bedroom and tried to talk to me. I was shaking so bad I couldn't even answer. I was sure she'd walk away and never come back. Instead she crawled in bed next to me, put her arms around me, and told me she loved me and would never leave me. That's when all the pain came out. I bawled like a baby. That was the day I started to heal.

Neglect comes in many forms. Perhaps one of the following is similar to what you experienced.

MISSING IN ACTION

Whether it was because of death, divorce, or poor choices, if you had a parent or spouse who simply was not there when you needed him or her, you have some grief work to do before you can heal. A parent or spouse who is not there *is not there.*

When a spouse or parent chooses to leave the scene, the remaining spouse and children are left to pick up all the heavy responsibilities. The abandoned spouse must take care of herself and her children alone without a partner to comfort or love her. This betrayal causes added stress on the entire family.

When a parent is not physically present, children lack a role model for what it means to be a woman or a man, a wife or a husband, a mother or a father. If divorce or poor choices was in the picture, the child has to face the fact that something else was more important to your parent than you were. Maybe your parent sent money but abandoned all other responsibility. Perhaps your parent walked out of your life, never came back, and you don't know why.

It is always difficult for spouses or children who have been left behind not to blame themselves. But the fact remains, the spouses or parents who left made a choice to abandon us and their responsibilities, and it was not our fault. Of course, if the spouse or parent died, he or she did not choose to leave, but many of the consequences for the survivors are the same. Sometimes it helps to remember that we are the only people who will never leave us. After taking the time to heal, we can survive, thrive, and live the rest of our lives with dignity and joy.

Emotionally Distant

We might have a parent or partner who was physically present but emotionally distant because of mental health challenges, addictions, or lifestyle choices. Because of this emotional distance, we might not have been able to form a meaningful emotional bond with that partner. We might not know that we have great value. We developed a false sense of who we are. We might not know that we have innate dignity. When we internalize these truths for ourselves, no one can ever take them away ever again. We can learn to treat ourselves with respect even if no one else has done so in the past.

Toxic Drama

Some marriages are toxic, and the children don't have a way to run from the constant poison. After we become adults, however, we have a choice to stay or not. If we remain in a marriage relationship where we are not treated with kindness and respect, we choose to keep getting hurt. We also choose to hurt our children. The greatest gift we can give ourselves and our children is a safe place to live and all the time needed to heal. We can't do that if we remain embattled in a family war.

Parents, siblings, and spouses who cause constant drama are

so wrapped up in their own needs, problems, and addictions that we cease to be actual people in their eyes; we become an object to control and manipulate. We are only useful when we provide what the parent or spouse wants. Our needs are not important. Neglected children and spouses soon learn not to have needs. They lose the ability to think about what they want, let alone ask it. They see their role as the person who must supply what the parent or spouse demands.

One man said,

> My father traveled a lot. I don't remember him being around much. I felt bad about that, but I got used to it. When my parents divorced, I didn't know the reason. My family was very good at keeping up appearances. When I got older, I learned that my father was living a double life, one with me and my mother and another one with his mistress and her daughter. I felt so betrayed. I don't think he ever thought about how his actions would affect me. It was hard to accept that I didn't matter to him. Every good memory I have with him felt like a lie. I think the greatest abuse and neglect is when a man or woman lies to his partner and children and lives a double life."

LACK OF AFFECTION

Healthy loving parents and spouses are affectionate with their children and partners. They play with them, touch them, hug them, kiss them, talk to them, and spend time with them. This inability to see the child or spouse as a precious unique person with the need to be loved and nurtured is never seriously considered by those who neglect. The lack of physical affection can be more damaging than outright abuse. Touch-deprived children and spouses are more anxious, apathetic, aggressive, or withdrawn. When no healthy physical affection exists in the home, children and adults are more insecure. Both children and adults need daily physical affection. Children deprived of touch actually become touch avoidant as adults.

Financial Neglect

Some choose to financially neglect their spouse and children. If we marry and bring children into the world, it is our obligation to do all we can to provide for our partner and children. We are responsible to provide for our family's needs.

One woman spoke of her financially neglectful parents this way:

> My mother and father used to "borrow" all the money I'd earned from all my babysitting and part-time jobs when I was growing up. They never paid me back. They always had trouble paying their bills because they were constantly overspending. I could not move out because they kept "borrowing" all my savings.

Another woman said this about her husband's financial neglect:

> My husband has an MBA but has not worked for seven years. He keeps looking for the perfect job and won't lower his standards to accept anything less than what he thinks he's worth. Our family has had no financial security. I've had to take over that responsibility myself. He has lots of excuses.

Making the Decision to Leave

Many questions must be considered before leaving a relationship. Most of us have worked long and hard trying multiple options to improve our relationship. Many of us have looked for solutions through counseling and medication. Others have tried to endlessly self-improve. It might help to consider the following question in making a relationship decision:

> *If I stay in this relationship, do I have to relinquish my self-respect, dignity, safety, and mental well-being?*

No one is required to stay in a heartbreaking or soul-damaging relationship. It is possible to walk away without guilt, for many feelings masquerade as guilt. Much of what we think is guilt is actually fear and longing—fear that our abuser will try to harm us for leaving and longing for the loving relationship we desired but never experienced. Walking away is not giving up on our abuser. Walking away from someone with a long pattern of abuse and neglect is walking toward accountability and healing for both the abused and the abuser. A destructive relationship will never be right if we never address the wrong.

All of us who have experienced abuse and neglect have struggled with the painful decision to end a relationship. We often leave and return numerous times hoping things will get better. Leaving is never an easy decision. Yet at some point we have to face the facts. The person who abuses and neglects us has already proven they are not worthy of our trust. It is more important to be trusted than to be loved. Trust is earned. We do not need to live with or associate with those we cannot trust—no matter how much we love them.

Healing does not come until there is safety from further abuse and neglect. When we are mentally, emotionally, and spiritually healthy, we will discover opportunities to practice loving and being loved with someone who is mentally and emotionally healthy enough to practice loving us back. By loving and being loved, we write a new chapter in our life that turns the tide of our tragic plot.

Now we need to earn our own trust. If we have been involved in a destructive relationship for a long time, we don't trust ourselves. We don't trust ourselves to keep us safe from further harm. Even if someone tells us we need to leave, we won't stay away from damaging associations until we face our Goliath of fear alone and become our own hero.

In the classic biblical tale of David and Goliath, David is a young man small in stature when he faced a giant Philistine warrior in the opposing army. David had no armor. His sling and stone were the point of derision, taunting, and laughter by the opposing forces. But after Goliath fell, David became a model of courage and the king of Israel. Our children and our children's children need us to be their David.

Questions to Answer

Answers to the following questions help us understand what happened while we were growing up or what is happening to us today. If we remember and acknowledge that we have been abused and neglected, we may be surprised at the mixture of emotions bottled up inside us. This inner confusion affects everything we do. When we understand where our feelings are coming from, we will understand ourselves with greater clarity. It helps to select a friend or therapist to talk to while we are remembering because we will feel the pain we have been denying or hiding for a long time.

Acknowledging and responding to the abuse and neglect we have experienced will allow us an opportunity to have a more fulfilling life. We can stop blaming ourselves for something we had no control over. We can respond to mistreatment with greater self-awareness and wisdom. Peaceful, loving, and uplifting relationships are possible for all of us.

- Do I feel invisible to my parent or partner?
- Do I try to win my parents or partner's approval and never receive it?
- Is my parent or partner a perfectionist?
- Am I punished by my parents or partner if I don't do everything their way?
- Does my parent or partner hug me or kiss me?
- Do my parent or partner threaten or frighten me?

- Does my parent or partner make fun of or belittle me?
- Did I feel safe in my home?
- Does my parent or partner do his or her part in providing adequate clothing, medical care, and educational opportunities for me and my family?
- Did I live in a dangerous place?
- Does my parent or partner fight and argue often?
- Is my parent or partner always busy or preoccupied?
- Does my parent or partner take time to be with me?
- Does my parent or partner often leave me alone?
- Does my parent or partner ever hold or comfort me?
- Does my parent or partner seem distant and detached?
- Does my parent or partner have an addiction?
- Has my parent or partner had an affair?
- Did my parent or partner abandon me?
- When do I feel most alone or scared?
- Did my parent use me as a confidante in their marriage relationship?
- Did I often feel like I had to be the parent to my parent?
- Did my parent seek emotional support from me?
- Was my parent or partner overly possessive of me?
- Does my parent or partner seldom allow me to try new things?
- Did I feel like the parent when I was a child because I was asked to accept adult responsibilities?
- Does my parent or partner criticize the way I look?
- Is it impossible to please my partner or parent?
- Do I get the impression that no matter what I do, my parent or partner will never approve of me?

- Does my parent or partner seem distant or aloof?
- Is my parent or partner overprotective?
- Did my parent or partner force me to live in an environment of marital conflict, domestic abuse, and neglect?
- Is my parent or partner preoccupied with his or her own problems and needs?
- Do I often feel lonely?
- Did my parent or partner tell me that I am worthless, that I would never amount to anything, or that I'd never do anything that would impress them?
- Does my parent or partner make fun of me or make me the object of jokes or put-downs?
- What effect has abuse and neglect had on my life?
- Do I want this pattern to continue?
- What am I going to do differently about my circumstances now that I understand the consequences of neglect?

Section Two

RESPONDING TO NEGLECT

Chapter Three

TYPES OF NEGLECT

Neglect is sometimes unintentional and sometimes deliberate, but it is always a pattern of destructive behavior by parents or partners who hold great power over those they might have loved. Our most important responsibility is to respect and cherish our partner and children along with sacrificing our time, talents, and resources for their welfare. When we neglect those who have willingly placed their hearts in our hands, we do harm that can last for generations. No other responsibility is more important than our relationships with our partner and children. No other accomplishment can compensate for our failure to love and care for those who depend on us.

The following is just a sampling of several types of neglect.

Rejecting

- any behavior that communicates abandonment, indifference, or not being wanted
- parental or partner emotional detachment
- refusal to show physical affection
- no positive praise or encouragement

- constant negative communication
- refusal to talk or communicate

Isolating

- preventing participation in normal social opportunities
- failure to provide a safe, loving home
- providing a home that a partner or child is embarrassed to show to friends
- refusal to allow friends in the home
- constant family chaos and negative drama
- forcing children to take on adult responsibilities so they have no outside recreational activities and social interactions
- ordering a child or partner out of the house

Terrorizing

- threatening abuse or abandonment
- providing a home with a climate of fear
- allowing a family member to abuse or neglect a partner or child
- leaving family members to fend for themselves for days, weeks, or months
- leaving a child alone with someone who is known to be abusive

Ignoring

- scarce parental or partner availability
- unresponsiveness to a child or partner's emotional needs
- failure to respond to a child or partner's urgent medical needs
- allowing work, sports, or church work to take priority over partner and children
- failure to initiate positive contact

Corrupting

- encouraging false values
- teaching antisocial or deviant behavior
- involving family members in criminal/immoral activities
- allowing abuse of a child or partner
- refusing family members the right to participate in religious activities

Limiting possibilities

- taking harmful drugs when pregnant
- providing inadequate nutrition
- administering harmful drugs to dependents
- limiting educational progress
- causing lasting deformities or conditions from lack of medical care

EXCUSES FOR NEGLECT

Everything we do is to satisfy powerful psychological needs such as the need to feel valued, loved, or at peace. The mature way to fill those needs is to focus on the needs of those around us. Not understanding the true nature of love, those who abuse and neglect focus exclusively on their own needs or their desire to be in control. When we are focused on ourselves, we are blind to the needs of others. As a result we miss opportunities to love and care for the people who live with us. We don't want to see our own negligence, so we don't. We spend our time creating lists of family members' inadequacies and develop mental blinders or excuses because we don't want to admit that we are neglecting those who depend on us.

Living an authentic life requires that we take responsibility for our ability or inability to love and be loved right now. We become adults when we fully understand that we are always responsible for how we act, no matter how we feel. We stop the blame game. Endlessly blaming and accusing others for our unhappiness is an empty way to love. Many of us spend a lifetime feeling short changed because others do not love and care for us the way we want to be loved and cared for; or we are blind to those who are dying for our love right in our own homes.

Those around us become real as their dreams, hopes, concerns, and their losses become as important to us as our own. Those of us who abuse and neglect are so absorbed in our own needs and demands that others become mere objects we manipulate and control to get what we want.

We are more likely to abuse and neglect others if we

- were abused and neglected as a child
- are keeping secrets
- have poor self-esteem
- are isolated

- lack support
- have unrealistic expectations of children or partners
- perceive our child or partner as handicapped
- think the child or partner reminds us of someone we don't like
- are dealing with an unwanted pregnancy
- are unhappy in our marriage
- are experiencing financial pressure
- have an addiction
- have lost employment
- are divorced

CAUSES OF NEGLECT

One of the major causes of neglect is parental or partner mental health issues. Substance abuse, domestic violence, unemployment, poverty, depression, and unintended pregnancies are other precursors of neglect. Neglectful partners and parents often exhibit the inability to plan, have no self-confidence, and often have difficulty handling money. They display emotional immaturity and lack knowledge of a child or partner's needs. They may be overwhelmed with the number of children in the home, lack resources, and often don't know how to effectively deal with stress.

On the news one day I heard an adoptive mother's plea for her son to give himself up after escaping from jail. A caring foster parent, she adopted him when he was seven.

> "His natural mother neglected and abused him," she said. "He was all ready to go back home when his mother said she didn't want kids anymore. That is when he changed. He started stealing and breaking into cars and was prosecuted when he was eight. We took him to psychiatrists and psychologists and all

> kinds of programs, and no one could get through to him. Not having someone who truly loves you and cares for you as a child can put someone on the wrong path.

Though we neglect each other for many reasons, we don't have adequate excuses to do so. When we attempt to justify or minimize our actions or inactions, we do not understand the long-lasting damage we cause or the hearts we break. The mistreatment of others cannot be justified. Neglected children grow up to be adults who have attachment difficulties, cognitive deficits, and emotional and behavioral problems. Insecure or anxious attachment in infants will affect their ability to attach to their partner and children in the future.

If we want to stop the mistreatment, we need to look in the mirror. We are the only people we can change. No matter what has happened to us in our past, our children and partners should not be ignored, neglected, abused, molested, abandoned, or estranged. The pain we have experienced gives us the power to understand how to ease the pain in others.

The cumulative effects of rejection and neglect are impossible to measure. The pain, suffering, undeveloped talents, and lingering mental and spiritual burdens should never be minimized. Children who were mistreated often develop problems when they are adults, such as eating disorders, tendencies for suicide, school or employment difficulties, and marital problems. Many who have been neglected have hard time adjusting to the stress of adult life and some choose to remain victims for the rest of their lives.

The Mind/Body Connection

Our bodies and minds work together in magnificent ways, yet this mind/body connection harms us when abuse and neglect are part of the picture. Our brain continually monitors our environment and the people around us for our personal safety. This is how we stay alive. Self-preservation is a powerful primal need that drives most of our behavior. We all develop strategies to stay alive when we are children. If we have been abused and neglected, those strategies are no longer an effective way to cope with the daily stress of adult life.

The need to feel safe, secure, and loved is especially critical in the early years of life because our brains are still developing and forming intricate connections. The chemicals in our brains are changed in response to our environment. Caregivers help form the chemistry and connections in the brains of those they care for. For example, when we see something that frightens us, our brain tells our body to secrete chemicals and hormones that help our muscles to tighten and our heart to beat faster, preparing us for flight in response to danger. Imagine the impact on the young child's developing brain when these same chemicals and hormones are introduced into the body without the ability to run from danger over and over again.

Adults in destructive relationships also have unhealthy chemicals and hormones released into their body on a continual basis. The consequences of this inner trauma are spiritual, emotional, physical, and social. On the other hand, loving, comforting, and soothing behavior on the part of caregivers or partners also changes brain chemistry and tells the body to secrete feel-good chemicals and hormones. Safe, secure, and loving environments are essential for normal growth and development in both children and adults. Neglect of children and partners causes long-term destructive consequences. When we betray and neglect our children or partners, we start of chain of mistreatment that will continue for generations.

REPORTING NEGLECT

Physical neglect is easier to document than emotional neglect, yet both are equally damaging. Children can be removed from a home and placed in foster care when they are in danger or where their basic needs are not being met. The court system and social service workers in these cases will schedule follow-up doctor and counselor appointments for the children. Parents will be allowed visitation and will also be given access to counseling and therapy to help them prepare for the return of their children. If parents do not follow court ordered instructions, their children will be removed from their home permanently and will be available for adoption.

Emotional neglect often goes undetected because it is easier to ignore and more difficult to document. A child doesn't know what he is living with is not good for him because he has never experienced anything else. When children are emotionally neglected, they feel alone, afraid, and depressed. Functional, loving parents respond to their child's fear and sadness with concern and comfort. Neglectful parents respond with anger, disgust, and more abandonment.

When we know or suspect a child is being abused and neglected and do nothing, we are part of the problem and share part of the blame. We can't step back and assume someone else will do something. In fact, we can be prosecuted when we are aware of cases of abuse and neglect and take no action. While covering up the ugly truth seems easier, in the long run, it is much more difficult. Abuse and neglect are like a sliver in society; the problem keeps getting worse until we remove it. We must be aware and watchful. Reports of possible abuse and neglect situations can be given anonymously if necessary. We can all do more to stop abuse and neglect.

Types of Spouse Neglect

Many married individuals find themselves alone most of the time while their spouses are involved in work, sports, TV, computer games and online social networks, Internet searches, and church or volunteer work. Of course sometimes couple time is at a premium, yet we should never minimize the importance of the time we spend with our partner. Too many partners feel starved for attention and affection. A strong marriage that will endure is one where spouses spend time together, are committed to the relationship, communicate, deal with problems in a positive way, give each other compliments, and share similar values. Yet some spouses prioritize little or no time for their partner. They don't just habitually forget birthdays or anniversaries; they abandon and neglect.

Many individuals don't admit that they are neglecting their spouses. They make no personal sacrifices to place the needs of their partner above their own. They believe they have valid reasons for being away most of the time. Common excuses include

- "I work hard all week and deserve time with my friends."
- "I'm doing God's work."
- "I deserve my downtime."
- "I only work long hours to provide for our financial security."

Our partner deserves our first priority. We are responsible to look after our partner's physical, spiritual, and emotional needs. The way we treat our spouse and children will likely be the way they treat their spouse and children. Destructive family relationship patterns move quickly from one generation to the next until we stop them. Our own private piece of heaven or hell is experienced right here on earth as the outcome of relationship patterns we began or perpetuated. We will eventually observe how our children treat our grandchildren and how our grandchildren treat our great-grandchildren. Then we will fully comprehend that our personal behavior continues in the lives of our posterity. What matters most in this life is how we treat each other, especially those in our own homes.

Neglect in adult relationships is an obvious cause of divorce. One way marriage partners neglect each other today is by obsessively using modern technology. Too often we allow digital distractions to take first priority. With excessive video gaming, online socializing, and web browsing, husbands or wives can waste hours, delay school or employment advancements, and sacrifice family relationships. Virtual friends become more important than family members. Spouses can become so addicted to texting, online social networking, and other uses of media and the Internet that they dismiss real partner-to-partner communication. Neglectful spouses allow the digital world to dominate their life. At first the time spent with digital devices seems harmless or is viewed as merely a few minutes of relief from the pressure of a hectic day. Yet important opportunities for one-on-one time with family members are missed.

Even beneficial forms of entertainment or recreation can become addictive and lead to the neglect of partners and children. Obsessive use of anything, such as gaming, television, movies, computers, or sports, leaves little time to communicate, lighten burdens, or build loving relationships. Even normally beneficial activities like practicing a musical instrument or exercise can become excessive and take precious time away from forming loving relationships.

ADDICTIONS

Addictions are a major cause of both child and spousal neglect. Alcohol, drugs, shopping, and pornography are common addictions.

One young woman expressed her feelings about her husband's porn addiction this way.

> My fiancé told me he had a pornography addiction in the past but that he had resolved the issue and did not engage in that behavior any more. I didn't understand addiction at that time

> and felt confident that this would not be an issue after we married. About the time I got pregnant, he returned to viewing pornography. I was the one who discovered the problem. Now he displays flash anger or comes home and locks himself in the bedroom with the computer. I can't tell you how devastated I feel. If I stay with this man who I love, do I have to have to deal with his addiction for the rest of my life?

The National Coalition against Pornography lists these warning signs of pornography addiction:

- Loss of interest in sexual relations or insatiable sexual appetite
- Introduction of unusual sexual practices in the relationship
- Diminished emotional, physical, social, spiritual, and intellectual intimacy
- Neglect of responsibilities
- Increased isolation (late nights on computer and withdrawal from family)
- Easily irritated and irregular mood swings
- Unexplained absences
- Preference for masturbation over sexual relations with spouse
- Unexplained financial transactions
- Sexual relations that are rigid, rushed, without passion, and detached.

Though largely a male addiction, pornography is also becoming a female addiction. Any person or image that a marriage partner turns to for sexual fulfillment instead of his or her spouse is destructive and the epitome of neglect. Our responsibility as mothers and fathers, husbands and wives, should be more important to us than any other interest in life.

Elder Neglect

The failure of a designated caregiver to meet the physical and emotional needs of a dependent elderly person is called elder neglect. Elder neglect may be unintentional and come from ignorance of proper caregiving or an inability to provide the care needed. To qualify as neglect, the caregiver knowingly withholds the basic needs of those who depend on them for that care. Elderly people are especially vulnerable to their caregivers because many are functioning on the level of a child. Neglect is intentional and includes the withholding of needed medication, nutritious food, and a clean healthy living environment.

Those who are elderly can also be physically abused or neglected much like a child with hitting, slapping, sprains, abrasions, fractures, bruises, or burns. They can also be emotionally abused or neglected with verbal outbursts, insults, name-calling, and threats of abandonment, or placing the elderly person in a rest home. Elders may also have their money, government checks, pensions, or property stolen or mismanaged. Elders may be asked to sign changes to their wills or other legal documents under coercion.

Signs of Elder Abuse

- Untreated bedsores
- Unsupervised dementia patient
- Lack of medical aids (glasses, teeth, medications, hearing aids)
- Lack of hygiene
- Lack of food
- Lack of proper housing
- Lack of clean clothing

- Unable to understand but forced to sign property transfer, power of attorney, or new will
- Caregiver has control of elder's money but won't provide for vital needs
- Excessive financial reimbursement or gifts for needed care and companionship
- Lack of necessities victim could afford
- Caregiver is verbally aggressive
- Caregiver isolates elder
- Unexplained changes in behavior
- Withdrawal from normal activities
- Unexplained changes in alertness
- Unexplained fractures, bruises, welts, cuts, sores, or burns.

REWRITING OUR STORIES

Abuse and neglect are often tolerated or hidden because we want to "look good" to outsiders. Both abusers and the abused keep secrets. Some religious individuals misunderstand the patriarchal order and believe their family must submit to unrighteous dominion. Many who tolerate abuse and neglect think their belief system requires them to be "obedient" to the person who abuses or neglects them. Some believe that ending a marriage relationship harms their ability to have a happy life after death.

Once we fully comprehend the devastating consequences of abuse and neglect, we can make informed choices and get outside help. The success rate of families with a history of severe abuse and neglect is low, even after treatment. Those who remain in destructive relationships risk their very lives. Being long suffering about abuse and neglect is not a virtue. Staying with someone who injures and ignores us is not in the best interest of anyone. It is not virtuous to allow abusers to hurt us or our children.

In the science fiction tale *Star Wars*, Luke has to face the difficult reality that his father is a man who has chosen the dark side and a man who has chosen to hurt people. In this story, the forces of the darkness are great and powerful and the forces for good are small and outnumbered. Luke must choose. Will he join with his father or become a force for good? Will he become part of the dark side or fight for the right against all odds? The fate of the universe hangs in the balance.

The fate of *our* universe still hangs in the balance. Each time we have been harmed and yet choose not to harm, each time we are not loved and yet choose to love, each time we are in pain and yet choose not to inflict pain, each time our hearts are broken and yet we choose not to break hearts, we ignite a light of love that can cast away the darkness. Sometimes we have to leave our home, to find our true home. We have to leave the false love we have known to discover real love. Empathy, warmth, compassion, and charity are the most powerful forces in the world. When we join our heart to these forces for good, we will someday receive the crown of a conquering hero. We can create a life of love.

Chapter Four

RESULTS OF NEGLECT

We all need human connection. We live out the story of our lives in relationships. Our very nature is to love and be loved. Infants in overcrowded orphanages actually die from the lack of loving touch and the opportunity to bond with one other person who truly knows and loves them. We all need more than basic food and shelter; we need someone who really cares about us. We all need certain nurturing experiences from those closest to us in order to thrive and develop the capacity to love. When we are loved, we have the opportunity to develop empathy. Our capacity to love originates from our ability to empathize or care about what it feels like to be the other person. It is difficult for a human being to love someone if they have never been loved.

Everything is linked into our ability to love and be loved—our health, productivity, creativity, and our very humanity. The history of our relationships with others dictate who we are today. Babies learn to care for others as they are cared for by others. Then those babies grow up and become us. Until we as caregivers learn to prize human goodness, humility, service, and charity above possessions, power, or prestige, we will neglect those closest to us and the cycle of man's inhumanity to man will continue in families, communities, and nations.

When children are neglected, they develop a wide spectrum of mental health issues. For example, most of us experience some mild depression and anxiety in relation to the ever-changing stressful events of our lives. Those of us who have been abused or neglected often struggle with mental health concerns that are not connected to our present circumstances. Some experts theorize that issues such as obsessive-compulsive disorder develop from the repression of our emotions in childhood. Repression is subconscious and results when an emotion rises inside us and a force stifles that emotion. Buried feelings don't disappear. Hidden emotions continue to exercise great influence on our subconscious and they later become apparent in personal symptoms that are extreme, irrational, and compulsive.

Results of Repressing Emotions

All emotions are good and help us develop mental wholeness, completeness, or maturity. When we consider an emotion bad or dangerous, we set the stage for repression. When an emotion is repressed by fear or shame, it is pushed to the subconscious, where it is buried. We no longer have conscious access to that emotion so we can deal with it constructively. Over time, these repressed emotions try to come into awareness. Sometimes we become obsessed with what we have repressed. For example, those who have repressed sexual feelings might later find themselves obsessed with sexual thoughts, porn, masturbation, sexual fantasies, and affairs. Those who have repressed feelings of fear may become obsessed with cleanliness or food intake and develop obsessive rituals characteristic of germ phobia, anorexia, or bulimia.

Most of us are comfortable with emotions such as yearning, hope, courage, joy, or love, but we are uncomfortable with despair, fear, anger, sadness, or hate. We repress these emotions at the cost of a healthy mental life. When we are not compassionate with our inner reality and allow ourselves to feel all our emotions, we become overwhelmed with guilt and shame, which quickly move us to repress any feeling that make us feel uncomfortable. Yet we can learn a great deal from raw emotion. Digging deeper to become consciously aware of what emotions we are repressing can be incredibly healing. As we learn to know and accept ourselves, even the dark and dusty corners of our soul, all our emotions become mentors or guides. If we can feel the full spectrum of our emotions without shame or guilt, we can wisely choose to express our feelings in ways that don't hurt us and those around us. Repressed feelings become obsessive. Felt emotions become tender teachers of our souls.

A good friend or therapist can help those of us struggling with mental health issues to identify repressed emotions. These people can give us permission to be aware of, talk about, and deal with *all* our feelings. If we can feel, we can heal. When we are aware of the full spectrum of our emotions, we can take an objective look at them and discover what they are teaching us. Then we can choose to express our feelings in meaningful and constructive ways. For healing to take place, we need to embrace, not repress, our emotions. We can be restored to a place of peace and wellness.

One woman I spoke with told me that she had been repressing feelings of anger for her parents because of their abandonment. Those repressed emotions kept creeping to the surface of her life in destructive ways.

> I spent most of my childhood in foster care. As an adult, I became obsessive and compulsive about cleanliness and my weight. I drove my husband and children crazy. I viewed myself as fat when I was actually thin. No one could keep my cleanliness standard, including me. I was always taught that you shouldn't even feel anger, let alone express it. I was taught that hating someone was a sin. I had repressed those feelings, but the guilt and shame remained and influenced everything in my life. I

> struggled with depression and anxiety. When I finally let myself feel mad at my parents, I could take an objective look at my feelings and finally let them go. I discovered that had a good reason to be mad, but what I really felt was sad, so sad even my bones ached. They abandoned me. I just couldn't stay stuck in mad and sad. After allowing myself to feel everything, I was able to finally accept that my parents were simply not mature or mentally healthy enough to take care of me. It was not safe for me to remain in their home because of my parents' choices, not mine. After that, the constant feelings of guilt and shame left for the first time. I didn't have to seek revenge because I had those feelings; I just had to acknowledge that I felt them. I had to feel the emotion before I could let it go. Then I could stop being so obsessive and compulsive.

How Neglect Harms Us

The greatest gift we have to give each other is our valuable time, positive attention, healthy physical affection, and unconditional love. When we deliberately deny those essentials of healthy living to those who depend on us, we break hearts and intentionally scar souls. When we hold the tender hearts of our children and partners in our hands, we are given a sacred trust that we violate at no small expense to our own humanity. It is impossible to harm those entrusted to our care without also harming ourselves.

Children are the most vulnerable to mistreatment. Children who are abused, abandoned, and neglected display huge gaps in normal cognitive development. They do not develop structures or pathways in their brains that normally form when children live with those who genuinely love and care for them. When you are forced to face the terrors of life on your own at an early age, you have no reserves to call on when dealing with difficult experiences. Instead, you are chronically overwhelmed and filled with anxiety and unexpressed emotion.

Children always blame themselves when they are ignored or neglected. This coping mechanism gives children the illusion that they have some control, when they really have little to none. It is almost impossible for a children to see their parents realistically because of innocence, naiveté, and lack of life experience. A child depends on his parents for survival. Facing the reality that your parent does not love you, wants to harm you, and is not there for you is simply too much for the child to bear and would overwhelm his psyche. So the child blames himself and eventually loses his ability to see or deal with reality.

One woman expressed her feelings as a child this way:

> When I was growing up, my mother always threatened to get rid of me when she was angry. She had these freak-out episodes. She would go after me with whatever she had in her hand at the time like knives, shoes, pans, or sticks. She used to whip my legs and buttocks with a willow until I had large red welts. Whenever she got in that black mood, I knew I was in trouble if I couldn't outrun her or hide. I remember hiding in the bushes in the backyard while she was looking for me and feeling warm, sticky urine run down my legs I was so scared of her. I became overly compliant as a result. I didn't do anything I thought might upset her. Even after I moved out, I did the same thing in all my relationships with other people in my family or at work. I never spoke up for myself and couldn't say no without feeling irrational fear. I couldn't do nice things for myself without feeling guilty. After I got married, the children came quickly. I was totally overwhelmed. I was close to a nervous breakdown before I realized something was wrong and I needed to do something about it. I didn't know how to take good care of myself. I had to learn.

Neglected children are starving guests at a banquet where they are not allowed to gather the emotional support, demonstrations of love, or attention and time they need to learn how to form normal mutually loving and healthy human relationships. This emptiness later develops into adjustment patterns to stress, such as learning and eating disorders, depression, and anxiety. Future social relationships are difficult because of lack of trust and underdeveloped communication skills. Those who are mistreated often develop healthy personal boundary issues and have low self-esteem. Many become socially isolated due to a deep-seated fear of rejection. Some are chronically angry. Others have lifelong mental problems or try to bury their personal pain in drugs, alcohol, or other self-destructive addictions.

More than half of the adults in the United States have experienced childhood trauma, which most certainly multiplies the rate of addiction, depression, anxiety, and suicide. There is a growing body of evidence that supports the idea that child abuse and neglect create fundamental changes in brain development. Some research studies suggest that nurturing and safety in infancy and childhood unlock certain genes that create self-soothing and self-regulating chemical receptors in the brain. These receptors help the body to quickly turn off cortisol production after a stressful event. Those who recover quickly from stress are able to avoid many diseases and mental disorders.

Other research suggests that some survivors of child abuse and neglect have greater difficulty with self-regulation, impulse control, physiological calming, and attention spans. This may result in erratic behavior, angry outbursts, inability to focus, mood swings, anxiety, depression, reckless behavior, failure to achieve goals, and hyperactivity. Some research also suggests that abuse and neglect in childhood result in multiple health issues when survivors reach adulthood, such as in increased risk for stroke, heart disease, cancer, diabetes, obesity, arthritis, headaches, alcoholism, illegal drug use, promiscuity, sexually transmitted diseases, and smoking.

Some researcher suggests that children who experience the trauma of abuse and neglect are often misdiagnosed with attention-deficit, conduct, and oppositional-defiant disorders, while others are misdiagnosed with mood disorders and anxiety.

Some are given antipsychotic drugs that have the potential to lead to suicide, loss of pleasure, weight gain, movement disorders, and diabetes. As a result, some researchers have been exploring alternatives to drugs with positive touch therapy and physical activities such as balance, posture, rhythm, breathing and motion, yoga, dance, music, drumming, exercise, horseback riding, and massage. These are attempts to rewire the parts of the brain that didn't receive the stimulation they needed at critical times in a child's development.

Others research reports positive results when survivors are exposed to treatment that includes hand-eye coordination, positive social interactions, lessons on understanding emotions, relearning how to trust, teamwork strategies, and how to watch for social clues. Some researchers suggest that survivors of neglect and abuse are moved along the path to healing by developing skills in meditation, mindfulness, positive thought patterns, and goal setting.

Though we all develop mental strategies to cope with stress in our life, those who stay in relationships where they are mistreated often develop unhealthy coping mechanisms such as the following:

Make-Believe Parents or Spouses

One way we deal with being neglected is by developing a make-believe caregiver or partner who is the opposite of the parent or spouse we really have. Children are able to do this because they are precious and innocent and they love their parents in spite of how they are treated. Adults are able to do this because they want their dating relationship or marriage to succeed at any cost. Children exhibit magical thinking or the ability to believe in someone without using logic. That is one reason why a neglectful parent can cause so much mental health damage. At some point, the magical thinking ends, and the child or spouse is left to face his or her dark reality alone. Parental or spousal abuse of power is the ultimate betrayal.

One woman told me she had created an imaginary father:

> I didn't realize I'd created an ideal imaginary father. It took me half a lifetime to finally accept that my mother was bipolar and had a violent, explosive temper. My father did nothing to protect me or my siblings. As a child, I imagined my father was Atticus Finch, the brave father in *To Kill a Mockingbird*. When I was in my fifties, the constant extended-family drama was seriously affecting my mental and physical health. The endless conflicts, threats, abuse, and neglect of my parents and siblings was taking me down a deep black hole—literally making me sick. So I decided to take some time off. I stopped initiating contact with my parents and siblings. That decision turned out to be such a gift. For the first time in my life, I felt safe enough to take a deep breath. Then dark memories began coming back into my consciousness from my childhood that I'd repressed. I had to grieve. Then I could learn how to think objectively about my extended family situation. I needed a safe distance from abusive family members before I could move forward with my life.
>
> After a few years of peace, I simply could not return to the family war. I had changed. I could no longer remain in any relationship where I was not treated with kindness and respect. My life today is *so* much better. In the past, I couldn't see abusive family members with any kind of objectivity. I feel like I've come out of a fog. I am finally able to admit to that the ongoing abuse in my extended family will end for me from this moment forward. Today I am able to forgive and love my parents and siblings, but I am not naive or stupid enough to trust them. I finally accept the fact that I can't fix my broken extended family. I now feel peace and joy every day of my life now. I don't know why it took me so long. I can focus on being the loving wife, mother, and grandmother my husband, children, and grandchildren need today.

Perfectionism

Another way neglected and abused children or spouses deal with destructive relationships is by becoming perfectionists. Perfectionism often develops as victims try endlessly to please an abusive or neglectful parent or partner. Children and partners who must "walk on eggshells" become their own inner critic and berate themselves for causing an abusive or neglectful episode. Or they cast themselves as villains who caused their parent or partner to abandon or neglect them. It becomes impossible to ever be good enough, attractive enough, smart enough, or anything enough. This effort to exert some control over our lives doesn't work and soon seems to prove to those who are abused or neglected that they are not worthy of love.

We do not have to be perfect to be safe and to be loved. We have the right to make mistakes. Our mistakes do not make us mistakes. Every mistake we make is an opportunity to practice loving ourselves in ways we've never been loved.

Typical excuses include:

- If I weren't so stupid, mommy wouldn't hurt me.
- If I weren't such a bad boy, my daddy wouldn't have left.
- If I get straight A's, keep my room clean, get into the right college, stop eating so much, my mother will finally think I'm good enough.
- If I just kept house better, he might want to be home more often.
- If I weren't so fat, she would want to be intimate with me.

Even after trying so hard, the hurting doesn't stop, the father never comes back, and nothing we do elicits praise. The child or spouse absorbs the shame and guilt for something she didn't do and something she can't fix. The tragedy is that this same scared and lonely child often grows up and becomes the abusive or neglectful parent because it feels normal. The lonely neglected spouse remains married but in a constant state of quiet desperation.

Self-Medicating

Another way we deal with abuse and neglect is by self-medicating. Buried emotions or pain often finds expression in physical maladies. Then we develop alcohol or drug addictions. Or we feel vague flu-like symptoms and feel chronically tired and achy all the time. When the doctors can't find anything physically wrong, they often write us prescriptions for antidepressants or other medications that help to further dull the emotions. Another way to self-medicate is by finding ways to numb-out so that we don't have to remember or feel. We unconsciously avoid pain by oversleeping, eating, shopping, exercise, or the excessive use of entertainment or electronic devices.

Compulsive Thoughts

One way we deal with the abuse and neglect issues in our lives is by developing repetitive thoughts and behaviors that keep us from thinking about and dealing with the big, scary, painful things we really don't want to deal with. The big, scary thing we don't want to face is the fact that someone we love doesn't love us. These compulsive thoughts and behaviors are a manner of coping, but they get in the way of a mature existence that is both full and abundant.

- "I'm bad."
- "I'm going to hell."
- "I'll never be good enough."
- "I'm a failure as a wife"
- "I wish I could die."

Addictions

Still another way we deal with neglect and the accompanying confusing set of unexpressed emotions is by developing any number of addictions. Excessive cleanliness, overwork, compulsive exercise, unnecessary risk taking, uncontrollable shopping, obsessive sex, alcohol, and pornography are common additions. Anything that causes stress can trigger these addictions. Being hungry, tired, lonely, or angry are feelings that often activate repressed pain. Those who are neglected will often crave something that will numb or take away the pain they are afraid to feel.

Self-Neglect

Many neglected children or spouses deal with their situation by becoming their own worst critics. Unfelt shame, depression, and fear are actually transformed into inner thoughts and images that are so terrifying and humiliating that they must be repressed before they trigger a compulsion to escape or act out the trauma with someone else. The original experience of parental neglect evolves into self-neglect. The very ability to stay supportively present for ourselves actually disappears. A chronic state of fear and depression are the result.

Those who have been neglected are more likely to neglect themselves or others because we only know what we know and usually do what was done to us. Because we had no power to make our parents love us when we were children, we often feel compelled to repeat childhood trauma by choosing relationships later in life with people who don't know how to love us. Why? It feels normal.

It is difficult to see that the trauma and neglect of our childhood has shaped our reality today. Both the negative and positive experiences of our youth have great power to influence our personalities, the people we choose for friends, the profession we pursue, our physical and mental health, the person we choose to marry, our appetite and addictions, the clothes we wear, and the way we behave in public and private. Our brains' mechanisms for responding to stress are programmed by the experiences we have in childhood. These experiences (whether remembered or not) influence our attitude, our behaviors, the way we see the world, the way we see ourselves, and the way we see others.

Relationship Problems

Many who have been mistreated develop unhealthy habits in all their relationships. A few examples follow.

Fighting

- feeling the constant need to assert self over others in an egotistical and entitled way
- displaying a chronic misuse of power or drive to misuse power to promote self over others

Fleeing

- an obsessive-compulsive craving to flee into any activity that numbs uncomfortable feelings or negates our ability to look objectively at reality
- displaying a lack of assertiveness and the constant need to avoid all conflict

Freezing

- the chronic inability to take any action to protect ourselves in a destructive relationship
- numbing or spacing out in ways such as oversleeping, over-fantasizing, or tuning out with television or overusing medications

Fawning

- abandoning our own needs by becoming subservient, submissive, compliant, and passive
- groveling to those who mistreat us.

UNDERSTANDING FLASHBACKS

Flashbacks are a common result of abuse and neglect. A flashback is a sudden emotional return to a traumatic experience. Most of us don't know that many flashbacks don't have a visual or even a memory component to them. In other words, people having a flashback don't realize they are having one. Instead, they experience a sudden burst of emotion unrelated to their current circumstances. For example, you are at the kitchen sink washing dishes when you suddenly feel terrified. Your heart pounds, your head spins, your hands shake, and you feel like you're going to die. These episodes are often called panic attacks. Almost anything can trigger a flashback, such as a certain smell or sound. This sudden emotional overreaction turns on the inner critic—"I'm going crazy. What is the matter with me?" Overwhelmed by the inner critic, we may become suddenly irritable, controlling, or pushy, or we feel driven by negative, perfectionistic, or catastrophic thinking.

On the other hand, we may find ourselves dealing with our anxiety attacks by choosing to numb out, flip on the TV, or browse the Internet. We choose to behave habitually in ways that help us become dissociated, spaced out, or sleepy. Or we choose to focus on solving someone else's problem by becoming the servant, self-rejecting, and groveling. All these examples are actually brought on by a flashback to the buried feelings in our past that are actually uncomfortable and unresolved feelings that we may not even remember.

A flashback can bring out physical responses in our bodies.

For example, our heart races, our pulse quickens, we feel like we are in danger, or we think we're going to die. We may feel suddenly sad and despondent with the accompanying physical symptoms of tiredness, foggy thinking, and desire to hide. If we can learn to tie these emotional flashbacks to childhood abuse or neglect, we have an easier time dealing with them in the present. The following are some thoughts we can use to replace unhealthy ones that flood our consciousness when we experience a flashback or anxiety attack.

- I'm having a flashback that takes me to a time when I was helpless. I'm not helpless anymore. These are past memories or feelings, and they can't hurt me now.
- I am afraid, but I'm not in danger. I am safe now. These feelings of fear will leave soon.
- I don't have to plan my escape. I do not need to hide. I am an adult with healthy boundaries now. I do not allow others to mistreat me.
- Something awful is not going to happen to me. I am feeling anxious and scared, but this feeling will pass if I allow myself to feel it.
- Take a deep breath and relax.
- I am good at keeping myself safe.
- I am a strong, assertive adult.
- I am kind to myself.
- I love myself.
- I am feeling sad, but I can count on myself for comfort and protection.
- What has happened to me in the past will not be what happens to me right now or in the future.
- I am a confident adult now with allies, skills, and the resources to protect me.

- I take good care of me.
- I can relax, slow down, and find a safe place to unwind.
- Fear is energy in my body. It won't hurt me if I don't run from it or react self-destructively.
- I will not be my own worst critic.
- I will not blow this situation out of proportion.
- I will stop the endless exaggeration of danger in my mind.
- I will stop trying to control the uncontrollable.
- I will no longer shame, hate, or abandon myself.
- I will not absorb unfair criticism or cave to unreasonable demands.
- I allow myself the opportunity to grieve. That means I will feel very sad right now, but the feeling will pass and I will feel better soon.
- I release unexpressed feelings of fear, hurt, and abandonment.
- I will turn my grief into self-compassion.
- I will turn my fear into self-protection.
- I will develop safe and loving relationships.
- I will take time to be alone and meditate.
- I will hand back feelings of shame to those who shamed me.
- I will avoid unsafe people, places, and activities.

When we pay attention to our feelings, especially those that seem to have no correlation to the reality of the moment, we become life puzzle solvers. At the moment we feel an emotion, such as fear, it helps to begin a kind and patient inner dialogue such as, "I am feeling afraid. Nothing in my reality at this moment is causing me to feel anxious. Perhaps I am having a flashback. I can feel afraid and not be overcome with it. This emotion will pass if I allow myself to feel it. I choose to be patient and kind to myself and those around me while I'm feeling this emotion." Trying not to feel our emotions doesn't work. Refusing to feel what you are really feeling is a form of self-neglect or abandonment. We can change this self-destructive pattern if we are aware of it and make a plan to change. On the other hand, we are always responsible for how we behave, and our feelings should not be used as an excuse for negative behavior.

Constant Feelings of Fear

We can become more aware of the moments when we are disconnecting from experiencing our emotions. This requires that we look more objectively at the way we chronically respond to emotions that we are uncomfortable with. One way we can do this is to become aware of our physical responses to internal emotions. For example, unacknowledged fear is often expressed as muscle tightness, nausea, jumpiness, shortness of breath, sweating, heart rate increases, hyperventilation, and diarrhea. When we experience these physical responses, it helps to ask ourselves what we are *really* feeling. For example, we could say this to ourselves, "I am terrified." Then we could find words of comfort such as, "I am terrified right now, but this feeling will pass if I allow myself to feel it," or "Right now, I decide if I need to move myself to a safe place. I am now an adult now who can protect myself."

Emotions can feel unbearable at first. Yet if we try not to be self-judgmental and stay true to ourselves, the intensity of these feelings will eventually lessen. Feelings of fear often trigger memories and unresolved grief from past abuse and neglect. Feeling what you really feel can bring these repressed feelings into consciousness. With practice these repressed feelings can be fully felt and gradually resolve into moods of relaxation and peace. When we experience the raw emotion, we also give ourselves the opportunity to reframe how we think about it. We each can be the person who comforts us now. When we finally and fully feel all our emotions, we will eventually be able to harvest forgiveness and self-acceptance from buried feelings of grief, pain, shame, self-doubt, and fear.

DISTORTED THOUGHTS OR IMAGES

Those of us who have been neglected have developed a mean inner critic who is always moving us to strive for safety and security though either productivity or perfection. We continually launch ourselves into a marathon of activity that keeps us one step ahead of fear, shame, and depression. Or we try endlessly to self-improve to the point of self-abuse. We are never good enough. Eventually unexpressed and unfelt emotions always surface. Sometimes they take the form or physical symptoms like feelings of heaviness, exhaustion, emptiness, hunger, longing, soreness, or achiness. Many of us unknowingly choose right-brain distraction or left-brain compulsive thinking. Both are masks we put on to cover sadness, loneliness, and grief we don't want to feel. The only healthy way to get through pain is to go through it; there is no way around. Avoiding pain is a major cause of mental illness.

DEPRESSION

Depression scares most of us. From all around us, we receive the message that we need to constantly feel happy. So what do we do if we really feel sad and scared inside? If we think we are supposed to be happy all the time, we add guilt to our sadness and fear. It is perfectly acceptable to feel scared or depressed at times. Those emotions are legitimate responses to many of the difficult experiences we have in this life. We just don't want to get stuck there. When we are feeling afraid and sad without an apparent cause, we need to take the time to examine what is going on inside our minds. Then we can invite certain thoughts to leave and welcome other thoughts to stay.

Sometimes we have a hard time naming or identifying our feelings, especially when we feel small, helpless, lonely, unsupported, unloved, and needy. Instead we camouflage our depression with other feelings. For example, feeling constant hunger even after a big meal is not physical hunger but emotional hunger. Feeling constantly alone even when we are around other people is not loneliness but often self-abandonment. Feeling constantly tired, but not from lack of sleep, is often caused by our inability to identify the real source of our pain.

In cases of severe depression, it is wise to consult a trained and licensed mental health professional. Some chemical imbalances may need to be treated with medication and cognitive therapy. Taking better care of ourselves is also helpful. It is important to make sure we have a healthy diet, daily exercise, and the proper amount of sleep.

One of the causes of depression is the negative audiotape of a toxic parent or partner constantly playing in our head, saying things such as, "You are stupid, worthless, useless, and ugly." We need to identify this inner critic and ask it to leave every time it invades our thoughts. We can develop the habit of living in a state of peaceful calm. Whenever we have a negative or fear-based thought, we lose the ability to think clearly. We give away our power when we allow these kinds of thoughts to remain in our minds. Once we learn to recognize a negative and fearful thought, we can work on quickly replacing it with a positive and hopeful one. We can take responsibility for the way we think. We don't have to be a victim of the negative emotions that result from our own negative thoughts. When we change the way we think, we reclaim our power to change the way we feel.

DISSOCIATIVE DISORDERS

Some of us who have been abused and neglected develop the mental disorders described below. Those who are abused and neglected often remain in a state of hyperarousal, or a state where the person is constantly anticipating threats. This state of anxiety can cause the child or adult to experience dissociation. The *Diagnostic and Statistical Manual of Mental Disorders* published by the American Psychiatric Association lists the following four common dissociative disorders.

Dissociative amnesia This condition is defined as memory loss not explained by a medical condition. For example, some people have no memory of their childhood or a certain period of their lives.

Dissociative identity disorder (used to be known as multiple personalities.) This condition is revealed by a switching of personalities when under stress. One or more "people" live and talk in the mind of the person with this condition. Partners and children of a person with this disorder are always walking on eggshells, never knowing which personality will act out from moment to moment.

Dissociative fugue (creating physical distance from your real identity or a sense of being detached from yourself.) People with this condition suddenly leave or travel away from themselves or forget who they are and adopt a new identity. This condition may last for a few hours or months.

Depersonalization disorder (a sudden sense of being outside yourself or observing your actions as if from a distance as though watching a movie.) With this condition, time may slow down, and color and shape may be distorted. This can last for a few moments or for years.

Knowing about these disorders can help us determine

whether we or a member of our family needs professional help. There is no shame in having a mental health issue, only tragic consequences when we don't get the help we need. When we seek professional help and take the responsibility to help ourselves, we are less likely to negatively affect the people closet to us.

Unhealthy Relationships

An unconscious part of us actually looks out in the world and locates the precise person who forces us to reenact our childhood trauma—another unhealed victim. If we were abused or neglected as children, we tend to choose to marry those who will abuse or neglect us or we find partners who will allow us to abuse and neglect them. Our subconscious really wants to heal the wounds of the past; but unless we are mentally healthy, we won't have the ability to choose healthy relationships. So we pick someone much like the caregiver who mistreated us. Then we bring children into the world with two parents who don't know how to love or be loved. That is how the pain of a loveless relationship moves from one generation to the next.

Genuine love, on the other hand, also moves from one generation to the next. We each can only be a transforming character in the lives of those who follow us after we have played that role in our own lives. We have the power to change not only our story but the stories of others by the way we respond to those who are wolves in Grandmother's nightclothes. A happily ever after story begins when one person makes the courageous choice to see reality and take action to change things for the better. We each have to be that person.

Little Red Riding Hood had to discern dark motives in her nemesis. What appeared as her loving grandmother was actually a wolf that planned to eat her. When she did not crawl in bed with the wolf but instead got suspicious and started making observations and asking questions, she took the first step to her own rescue.

"My, what big eyes you have."

"What big teeth you have."

The wolf always had a logical answer for each question, but Red soon learned that her observations were valid. Luckily a passing woodcutter aided in her rescue and later her grandmother was freed from the locked closet. Red's observations and questions beg us all to do the same. When we ask questions and doubt the sincerity of those who seek to harm us, we begin the rescue that will save future generations.

Questions to Answer

The results of abuse and neglect are profound and long lasting. We need to stop minimizing destructive relationships and change the way we respond to those who choose to harm us. Many of the negative thoughts we have about ourselves are the direct result of the mistreatment we experienced in a troubled childhood, dating relationship, or marriage.

After we remove ourselves from destructive relationships, it is important to remember that it takes time to heal the damage to our psyche. Healing takes time, and we need to be patient and kind to ourselves on the journey to wholeness. If we don't choose to heal, we will enter into other relationships where we are mistreated again and again. The following questions are designed to get us thinking so we won't repeat a pattern of abuse and neglect.

- Do I tend to love people who don't love me back?
- Do I always put others' happiness before my own?
- Do I feel like it is my responsibility to make other people happy?
- Do I believe I am unworthy of love?
- Do I constantly search for external validation to feel like I am good enough?
- Do I have a hard time expressing my wants and needs?
- Am I guilty, anxious, or scared?
- Do I think people would be better off without me?

- Do I have to be in a relationship to feel good about myself?
- Do I blindly obey the relationship rules forced on me without question?
- Am I afraid of my parent, partner, or family member?
- Do I allow my partner or parent to make all important decisions?
- Am I uncomfortable with conflict?
- Do I allow myself to be coerced, demeaned, dismissed, abandoned, abused, or neglected?
- Do I bury my hurt feelings?
- Do I often walk away from mistreatment issues because I am afraid of retaliation?
- Do I never/always buy things for myself?
- Do I find it hard to empathize with people?
- Do I feel like I will never be good enough?
- Do I have a hard time standing up for myself or saying no?
- Do I avoid feeling pain?
- Do I make excuses when my parent or partner is selfish and abusive?
- Am I afraid to live alone?
- Do I allow others to constantly criticize, bully, or threaten me?
- Do I long for peace?
- Am I afraid to leave a relationship because I don't want to be financially destitute?
- Do I put up with cruel behavior?
- Do I blame myself when there is friction in my relationship?

- Am I able to state my opinions and desires without fear?
- Do I respect myself?
- Do I see myself as irreplaceable and incomparable?
- Do I trust myself to leave abusive situations?
- Do I expect to be treated with kindness and respect

Section Three

Recovering from Neglect

Chapter Five

Overcoming Self-Neglect

We have two common responses to neglect. One, we become chronically self-absorbed and selfish in an effort to fill the needs our caregiver or partner did not fill. Or, two, we become so self-effacing and self-abandoning that we lose the ability to properly care for ourselves while caring for those around us. It is possible to care for ourselves without becoming selfish and self-centered. It is possible to fill our own needs without abandoning the needs of those around us. If we choose to care for both ourselves and others, we have the opportunity to develop mature loving relationships.

Results of Self-Neglect

Self-neglect often begins in childhood when we adapted or repressed our needs to fit the circumstances we lived in. We didn't understand why we were not important to our caregivers, so we assumed that we were the problem. Neglected children often become their own worst critics. This pattern repeats in adulthood. When a child is not loved, he is driven to seek attention and acceptance by becoming an overachiever, perfectionist, or a rebel. These patterns also repeat in adulthood.

One man expressed his confusion about his relationship with his mother this way:

> When I was growing up, I *never* remember my mother telling me she loved me, hugging me, or kissing me. I knew she was angry with my father for getting her pregnant, and the result of that was me. She always let me know how much I had ruined her life and talked about all the wonderful things she could have done if I'd never been born.
>
> I remember being left alone to fend for myself most of the day. Mom spent most of the time in bed. I look back now and realize she was depressed, but as a small child, I just thought she was sleepy. My job was to make sure I didn't wake her or make her mad. If I did she'd fly into a rage. I learned to take care of myself.
>
> My dad was never home. He traveled a lot with his work. I look back now and understand why. Mom was hard to live with: wide mood swings, volatile temper. Why he left me alone with her when he knew what she was like, I'll never know. They eventually got divorced, and I never saw or heard from him again. My mom blamed me for the divorce. She blamed me for everything.
>
> School was the only place I felt noticed. I got perfect grades, but nothing seemed to impress my mom. I got a full-ride scholarship to college, and then I started my own business. Now I'm a self-made millionaire, but nothing I do is enough for her. Mom lives with me now. She doesn't have anywhere else to go. I'm starting to avoid home because she is always on my case about something I'm doing wrong. I know how she treats me affects how my wife and children see me. It is easier to be a workaholic. I've been waiting my whole life for her to tell me she loves me and she's proud of me. My wife wants her out of our home. I don't want to throw her out. I feel trapped.

If we never received parental or partner approval, we often struggle to feel that anything we do is good enough. We become perfectionists who constantly feel like frauds because perfection is not possible. We don't understand that perfectionism is a form of self-abuse and that our negative labels are never accurate. Then we continue the destructive relationship patterns we have known by seeking attention in negative behavior or by withholding approval from ourselves and others. Eventually we become more and more closed off from life and struggle with depression and anxiety. Just because our parent or partner did not love us in the past doesn't mean we can't learn to love ourselves and others today.

Everyone needs acknowledgment, positive attention, affirmation, and affection. Without those elements of an abundant life, we are like flowers that whither on the vine for lack of rain and sunshine. For example, touch is absolutely necessary for a healthy, happy life. When we are touched, the amount of hemoglobin in our blood increases. Hemoglobin is the part of the blood that carries important supplies of oxygen to all the organs such as the brain and the heart. An increase of hemoglobin can also prevent disease and speed recovery from illness. The simple act of giving or receiving a hug can lift our spirits and improve our physical and mental health.

Learning to fill our basic nurturing needs while assisting others to fill their needs helps us to develop into mature and compassionate human beings. Saying a kind word, affirming someone's importance, or offering a pat on the back may seem like small gestures, but when they are missing from a relationship, both people are starving for love. Struggling year after year to receive love from someone who is not capable of loving us in return is an empty search that leaves us hungry for something we'll never receive. We forget there is a banquet of love within; we need only to reach out in love to those who are willing to practice the art of love with us.

Sometimes we unintentionally refuse to see the consequences of the destructive relationships in our lives. We choose to hang on to people who harm us at the cost of personal honesty, respect, and dignity. We gauge our decisions by how our abuser will respond. We sport a mask, play a false role, and hide or deny our true feelings. We say we're fine when we are not. We say we're not hurt when we are. We carefully ponder how our abuser will react before we say or do anything. It is time to stop allowing people who harm us to control our behavior, emotions, thoughts, and feelings—that includes members of our family. It is time to step out of the fog of this negative and dishonest way of living.

If we stay in destructive relationships long enough, our personalities never flower. Our personal likes and dislikes become irrelevant. We no longer see or our strengths and weaknesses. We become invisible. We behave only in ways that will keep the status quo. We exist only to appease the demands of our abuser. We feel successful only if we avoid an abusive episode by cowering and demeaning ourselves. We talk ourselves out of holding our abuser accountable because we are afraid to be alone or we don't want to lose our financial stability. Eventually we choose to face and leave the destructive relationship, or we choose to continue tolerating abuse and neglect. With the latter we choose a life of emptiness, fearfulness, self-blame, and shame.

Personal change is hard, but it is possible with even a seed of hope and an ounce of courage. Because we have no control over anyone but ourselves, all change starts with us. If we want to respect and trust ourselves, we need to change our response to those who harm us. We might inwardly tremble in the presence of an abuser, but we don't have to let that fear stop us from doing the right thing. We need to understand that roller coaster relationships are toxic and cruel. Then we can finally quit blaming ourselves, hand the guilt and shame back to our abusers, and expect them to take full responsibility for their choice to mistreat us.

On the other hand, perhaps we have become the kind of person who harmed us. We care only for our own needs. We control others with angry outbursts. We manipulate with threats and corrosion. We neglect those who depend on us and are unable to care for themselves. We consider only our own likes and dislikes. Those around us are merely puppets to control or force to our will. Or perhaps we don't want to face the pain of being unloved in our childhood, so we hold back our heart, never allowing others to get too close. This is also a form of self-neglect. We neglect to love and rescue the child who was us, the child who was abused and neglected. We soon discover we have no lasting power over others and feel empty and soulless.

Too often this self-neglect happens over and over. Our childhood experience of parental abandonment or neglect evolves into adult self-neglect. We lose the ability to be our own internal support system. Our mental and emotional health suffers. We don't see reality. Our inner world of thoughts and beliefs becomes a place to disassociate from the stark truth we don't know how to face. Not everything we face can be changed, but certainly nothing can be changed until it is faced.

What we don't want to face is this:

> The person I love doesn't love me.

It is devastating to love someone and not be loved in return, especially if that person is our parent or our partner. Consider the damage done to tender minds and hearts. Being neglected is particularly damaging to an innocent child. Because a child will die without his parents' care, he knows that he must give up his needs to conform to what his parents want. If our parent requires that we take care of him, we do it. If our parent is addicted, we cover for him. If our parent is irresponsible, we take on his responsibilities. If our parent is lazy, we become a responsible mini-adult. The child's needs are never addressed by the parent or the child.

Our parent's or partner's inability to love us affects us in profound ways. We soon learn to forget who we are and don't even know what we want. We lose the ability to act in our own best interests. We feel responsible to save our parents' dysfunctional marriage, or we are desperate to keep the family together at all costs. That is why those who are neglected and abused in childhood often have a difficult time breaking away from destructive family relationships even when they become adults. We feel responsibility to repair something we didn't cause and can't fix. It helps to understand that relationships in destructive families don't get better over time when abuse and neglect are tolerated.

Although we always take rejection personally, it is vital to understand that our parent's or partner's inability to love us has nothing to do with us. Their inability to love is not about us at all; it is about them. When we have been mistreated, we seldom recognize that the person who rejects us has a problem and we can't solve it. Even if we choose to leave our neglectful parent or partner, we often continue the abuse and neglect through the way we treat ourselves.

What we need to understand is that everyone is worthy of love. Love doesn't have to be earned. We all deserve to be loved. Just because the person we love doesn't love us back doesn't mean we're not worthy of love. On the other hand, trust is earned. It is better to be trusted than to be loved. An abuser can't be trusted. Confusing trust and love gets us all in a lot of trouble. One woman told me this story:

> I was sexually abused by my father from the time I was a little girl to the time I left home. My mother was addicted to pain medication and basically ignored me. She had this twisted image of men, and she taught me that they only want one thing from women. I guess this included my father because when I told her what was happening, she told me to never tell anyone or daddy would go to jail.
>
> Somehow I thought if I got fat, Daddy would stop wanting me that way because my mom was obese. So I overate until I looked just like her. The abuse didn't stop until I moved out and found my own apartment. Eventually I married a man a lot like my father. He wasn't faithful to me. We got divorced when I found out he was abusing my daughters. At least I stood up for

them. My mother never stood up for me. I'm over 300 pounds now. I guess my plan is working. No man has looked at me for years. Frankly I'm glad. I believe what my mother taught me. Men only want one thing from women.

I'm so exhausted when I get home from work, I turn on the TV and get out the snacks and plop down on the couch. Now both of my children are overweight too. Their father is out of the picture, and good riddance, but they need some positive male attention, and they aren't getting it. I don't want any more men in my life. My kids are acting out at school, and I don't know what to do any more. I feel like I'm lost inside this enormous body, a sad little girl just crying to be loved. But I know it will never happen.

FEAR AND DEPRESSION

Deciphering Depression

One of the results of self-neglect is a sense of hopelessness and depression. It's important to learn to distinguish between depressed thinking and depressed feeling. Depressed thinking can be lessened or eliminated with time and practice. Depressed feeling, on the other hand, often must be experienced before we can move forward. That is why depression might be thought of as a gift or an invitation to help us to grow. We may have been preprogrammed to think that feeling depressed is just another proof that we are less able to cope than others, defective, not good enough, unworthy, and unlovable. Feeling depressed can be a great gift if we use this inner oil gauge as a signal that our soul needs some maintenance.

One of the causes of depressed thinking is the obsessive perfectionist voice inside our head. This inner critic grows rampantly in abused and neglected children. Continuous mistreatment encourages the child to overdevelop hypervigilance and perfectionism to defend against perceived danger, win approval, and create safe attachment. But safety and attachment are not experienced even after these overzealous efforts. Hypervigilance evolves into intense performance anxiety. Perfectionism becomes a harsh inner voice that grows into self-hate, self-disgust, and self-abandonment at every mistake or imperfection.

Facing Our Fears

When a neglected or abused child becomes the adult, he or she is dominated by feelings of danger, shame, and abandonment. Most of us are unaware of the many community resources to help those who have been abused and neglected. Often we don't know that there are healthy people in the world who are capable of offering us love and acceptance. We live in a constant state of fear. We listen to the internalized voice of the toxic parent or partner in our heads. Catastrophic thinking and perfectionistic demands can be managed as we learn to manage our thoughts.

We can take back our power by changing the way we see ourselves. When we learn to see ourselves accurately, we will finally feel safe. Often we see others as a threat because we believe they can still hurt or demean us. Our subconscious mind thinks that our abuser's opinion of us really means something or that the negative things they told us must be true. Though it is difficult, when we finally acknowledge that these subconscious assumptions are false, we will finally feel safe.

Other people can think whatever they want. They can tell us that we are selfish, sinful, ugly, and rotten human beings. What others say does not change who we are. We are the same no matter what anyone says about us. We won't feel threatened by anyone when we realize that they can't really hurt us. What others think should never influence what we feel about ourselves. When we know that we are wonderful, good enough, and amazing human beings, then the constant fear that we aren't good enough will go away.

Our value is never on the line no matter what others do or say. Our lives are not a final exam but a continuous classroom for learning and growing. We are irreplaceable. Our soul is on a journey toward love. No one can diminish us, hurt us, or make us feel small without our permission. When someone "makes" us feel something negative about ourselves, it is because on some level we are afraid they are right. We believe we really aren't good enough. We see ourselves in a negative way. We lose our fear and others lose their control over us when we see ourselves as strong, valuable, and irreplaceable. We must know the worth of our own souls so deeply that no person or circumstance can take that reality away from us.

As we let go of fear, we can see our abuser more accurately. People who hurt other people are scared, deeply scared. They are just struggling to make their way in this world. Their behavior is driven by the fear that they aren't good enough. Their words and actions are about them, not us. When those we love abuse us, we can take a step back and choose to see the situation from their perspective. Abusers always make us out to be the bad guy so they can feel better about themselves. Just because abusers think they are right, it doesn't mean they are. Just because they say horrible things about us, it doesn't make it true.

We all cope with destructive relationships to some degree. Yet those who have been harmed by those who should love them most, like their partners and parents, are dealing with issues that are better addressed when they are acknowledged and understood. As we heal from fear and depression, we become who we really are—the precious souls we were before we were harmed by those who might have loved us. We feel our own value and learn to be as generous and kind to ourselves as we are with others.

One woman told me about a life-changing moment when she decided she was worth it:

I was fifty-eight years old before I ever went to the store, picked out exactly what I wanted, and paid full price.

On the way home, I said out loud, *'You are worth it.'* for the first time. That moment was a milestone for me. I'd never told myself that I was worth it before. I felt lighter somehow, as if I'd lost a hundred pounds. Before this experience, I'd always gone to the thrift store and bought the cheapest thing possible because that is the way I saw myself, worth little to nothing. I even felt guilty when anything good happened to me. My clothing and posture reflected how I felt inside. On the way home that day, I had a conversation with my dead mother. I told her exactly how I felt—something I'd never been able to do while she was alive. I was surprised to hear what I thought and how I felt. I finally decided to let go of responsibility to solve all the problems she had created while she was alive. I told her that I could not fix all the people she broke. I gave the problems she'd created back to her. I don't think I've ever felt so free before.

Re-Parenting Ourselves

It is possible to compassionately re-parent ourselves after we become adults so that we don't continue to suffer needlessly. Re-parenting means becoming the loving parent to ourselves that we missed in childhood. No one can make up for what we missed, not even our parents today. Yet we can practice thinking and talking to ourselves the way a loving parent would talk to us. We can give ourselves the safety and security we need to make mistakes and learn from them. Before we can re-parent ourselves, we must keep the following ideas in mind.

Stop Self-Blame

The way our caregivers treated us is not our fault. Their behavior is a decision they made. No matter what they said to us, we were not inadequate or unlovable. We are not bad or defective. We didn't deserve to be abused, abandoned, ignored, or rejected. We simply had parents or partners who did not know how to love and nurture us. While we may never know why our caregivers or partner behaved a certain way, we can rest assured that they probably did the best they knew how at the time. It is also possible that they were treated the same way as children.

Hand Back Shame

We are adults now, and we can understand this simple truth: how we are treated by others has nothing to do with who *we* are; it has everything to do with who *they* are. If we have been mistreated, our parents or partners let us down. We didn't deserve it and it is not our fault. Many who abuse and neglect their partner or children are mentally ill. Many who neglect others are struggling with undiagnosed and untreated depression.

See Our Parent/Partner Realistically

Previously we did not have the ability to see our parent or partner in reality. We were so desperate for our relationship to succeed that we were not capable of seeing them accurately. We saw ourselves as the problem. We coped with our situation by believing we deserved to be treated without kindness and respect. We concluded that we were not worthy of love. That was our way to cope with an intolerable situation. We tried and tried to become worthy of our abusers love—but that never happened. It is a healthy choice to remove ourselves from those who mistreat us. When we are mentally stable, we have the ability to choose to be around people who are capable of a healthy relationship.

We came to our parents and partners after they had

accumulated baggage from their past. We didn't cause their problems and we can't fix them. We don't have to be their judge and jury in order to remove ourselves from destructive relationships. We can forgive and feel compassion for our parents or partners even if it is not safe for us to have a close relationship with them right now.

Our Aspirations Are Our Possibilities

Many of us who have been mistreated have never developed our individual talents. Yet each of us has personal gifts, talents, and abilities that we can use to bless our own lives and the lives of others. We honor our own precious life by not neglecting these gifts. We can't live authentically if we don't trust our inner voice. Feeling inadequate is common to all of us, but these feelings must not stop us from developing into loving human beings. It takes courage to foster a talent or create a work without worrying about how it will be received. If our desire is to use our gifts to bless the lives of others, we will find fulfillment in this life.

Take the time to write down your dreams. Imagine your life in the future. Learn to listen to your heart. Pick up the brush, pen, or hammer. Give yourself quiet reflection time. Slow down. Try something new. Take time to be alone in nature and meditate. Notice what gives you peace and joy and fill your life with it. Seek more for serenity that security. The more we are grateful for, the more we will be given.

When others offer their opinion about us or our potential or our gifts, we can listen and weigh whether their insight is helpful to us or discouraging. If it is discouraging, we can let it go and move forward. There is a higher goal in life than appearances or possessions. Making a positive difference in our lives and in the lives of others offers us true satisfaction, joy, and peace of mind.

When we are truly interested in others, a graciousness and inner light comes from our countenance.

We all have a conscious mind that reasons for us and a subconscious mind where our emotions and creativity reside. Don't put your emotional or creative life on hold. Becoming a loving man or woman takes time; so be gentle and patient as you grow. It is necessary to think affirming things about yourself before you have the energy to try again and again. It is vital to nurture yourself with adequate sleep, exercise, nutritious food, and time for reflection.

We often depend on our parents and partner for encouragement before we take the initiative to accomplish our dreams and wishes. Though it is wonderful to have a positive parent or partner who inspires us to fulfill our dreams, it is not necessary. We can allow the needs of others to inspire us and become the person who helps others accomplish their desires as we do the same. One woman told me how she overcame the limits her parent placed on her:

> When I was in junior high, I asked my mother if I could play the violin in the school orchestra. She told me that only rich kids can do that. I believed her and sang in the choir because that didn't cost anything. It wasn't until I was in my fifties that I decided to listen to the desire to learn inside me. I learned how to play the violin and joined an orchestra. I can't express how much I love this. We give free concerts in our community, and I love it.

One man told me that he always wanted to be an author but had no encouragement from anyone and eventually gave up on the idea:

> I used to love writing as a child but had no encouragement from my teachers or parents. Finally I got tired or what others said I could or couldn't do. I started writing, and I haven't stopped since. I am now a published author of over a dozen books. I

> was true to the voice inside me that told me I had something important to say.

One woman shared her advice about developing gifts and talents:

> My mother was an artist who covered the walls of my childhood home. I desperately wanted to paint like her. When I asked her to teach me, she was always too busy. One day I finally talked her into letting me to touch her oil paints. Without any instruction, my first attempt did not amount to much.
>
> "Then my mother said, 'See I told you that you couldn't do it. Look at the mess you've made.' I felt too intimidated to ask for her to help me ever again. When I took my first art class in college, the instructor saw something in me that I did not see in myself. He told me that I was a true artist, and he inspired me. I am an artist now. I don't need anybody's permission anymore to follow my heart. Now when I get negative criticism, I look at it objectively and see if I can improve. But if the criticism is discouraging, I let it go."

It is time to make some wishes and then do what is necessary to make them come true. If we have positive thoughts about ourselves and others, they will shine from our faces in radiant smiles. If we explore our possibilities and we are willing to keep learning and growing, the person we become will illuminate the world. Others will perceive our light and be drawn to it. Unlike Aladdin, we don't need a genie to make our wishes come true. We are the genie. We make wishes come true.

When we give someone power to determine the outcome of our lives, we give up our very souls. No one can diminish us without our permission. The seeds to bless, uplift, and inspire reside inside our hearts, ready to blossom. We are shining, glorious souls. Health, creativity, and humanity are already ours. The depths of pain we have experienced have pushed us to become our highest selves. We have survived, and now we choose to thrive. We are free to live a life that matters—a life of love.

Chapter Six

AVENUES TO HEALING

One of the greatest gifts we can give ourselves is a safe, loving place to live. If we are not safe and loved in the place where we live today, something needs to change. If we live with those who abuse and neglect us, we can move or ask the person we live with to move. If we live alone, we can learn how to love and accept ourselves. Creating a loving home is possible for everyone.

Leaving abuse and neglect behind is like leaving the only home we've ever known and beginning a new life in a foreign land. We can choose to think about this change in the way we live and the relationships we engage in as an adventure or a calamity. There is always a learning curve when we try something new. It takes time and patience to get used to new ways of thinking and behaving.

In the same way we often use a guide when we visit a foreign country, we need others who have healed from mistreatment to show us where to go and what to do in this new place. Perhaps we aren't sure we want to live in this land because we've never been here before and we don't know what to expect. We wonder, "Is it really worth the difficult adjustments and sacrifices I have to make to change my life? Will a new home free from cruel relationships really be better than what I've known?"

Living in a home where we are safe and loved is possible for each of us even if it requires that we must be alone or penniless for a season. Creating a sanctuary without abuse and neglect is possible if we are willing to change our thought currency. For example, when we are guests in a foreign country, residents will tell us that we need to change the cash in our pockets because our money is of no value in this new place. Sometimes it is difficult to turn over what we have always considered valuable for something that looks like fake money to us. We have to trust that those who live in this new country are telling us the truth. Then we have to experiment with or use our new currency to see if it really works as promised.

Discovering New Love Currency

Sometimes when we visit a new country, we notice that families relate differently in other cultures. For example, maybe we are in a marriage or we grew up in a family with little or no physical affection. We can all learn to openly demonstrate physical and verbal affection without embarrassment. It might take time and practice before we get used to saying, "I love you" or offering a gentle embrace. Loving families openly express their devotion and often point out what they appreciate about each other. Loving families quickly apologize and express sorrow when they have behaved negatively. With practice and patience we can all get comfortable saying, "Thank you" or "I'm sorry."

One of the biggest thought currencies we need to change is constant self-blame. Even though it doesn't make sense to a rational mind, most of us who have been abused or neglected still hold on to some form of self-blame.

- "I never did anything to stop it."
- "It's my own fault because I chose to marry this person."

- "If I were a better child, my parents would not have treated me that way."
- "I deserved it."
- "It's isn't that bad. I should just put up with it."
- "It was my fault."

All abusers blame their victims or apologize profusely only to repeat the behavior in short order. Abusers don't want to feel their own pain so they blame those closest to them for their behavior, deviancy, or neglect. Common excuses include:

- "You push my buttons."
- "If you weren't bad I wouldn't have to do this."
- "Who would want to come home to you?"
- "You're worthless."
- "You aren't worth paying attention to."

If we want to live in a home where we are safe from abuse and neglect, we need to exchange this faulty pattern of thought for a different currency. This previously valued tender is of no value here and needs to be exchanged.

This is our new thought currency—*the way I am treated is not my fault.*

Those closest to us behave the way they do for a number of reasons. But remember, reasons for behavior are not an excuse. There is no adequate excuse for abusive or neglectful behavior.

This is another new thought currency—*the way I respond to how I am treated is my responsibility.*

Feeling guilty about being abused or neglected is normal even if it makes no sense. In fact, the mistreatment we experience is our partner's or caregiver's issue, not ours. It has nothing to do with us. Abusers always blame the victim and seldom take responsibility for their actions because they are past feeling and unable or unwilling to control themselves. Abuse and neglect continue to harm us if we continue to believe we deserve it or if we continue to allow it.

We have the responsibility to protect ourselves and those who depend on us. Letting go of people who mistreat us doesn't mean we or they are a bad people. It just means that it is not safe for that person to be part of our story anymore. If we want a happily-ever-after ending to our life, it is time to make it happen. Unlike what fairy tales would have us believe, no prince charming is waiting in the forest.

It takes courage to dramatically change how we've been responding to a destructive relationship. Something has to change before our lives can get better, and that something has to be us. Most people I've talked to wish they had taken corrective action sooner, before damage was done to the next generation. It seems easier to let things remain the same, but staying in a destructive relationship ultimately destroys both the abuser and the victim. Our potential for growth and development as a mature and loving human being is stymied by our choice to stay.

I often hear people say, "Why didn't you just leave?" or "Why didn't you tell someone?"

In truth, those who are abused and neglected don't know how *not* to stay. We learned in childhood to accept what is unacceptable. We learned to stay. We struggle with losing the people we deeply love. We don't know how to live differently. We need someone to show us the way. We need someone to give us hope that peace and joy will follow the struggle and loss of leaving those who harm us. We need someone to tell us that good can come from bad and that love is always the lesson.

We need someone who lives in safety and love to put her arms around us and say, "I'm so sorry that you have to lose the people you love because they don't have the capacity to love you back. I promise you that your choice to leave cruelty behind will change your life into one that is beautiful and meaningful. I promise you a new life with love and joy. I can't promise you a life without struggle and challenges, but I promise you a peace of mind and inner contentment and fulfillment you can only imagine today."

Even though abuse and neglect are two of the most devastating experiences, they can only destroy our possibilities for a meaningful life if we do nothing. We can end our abusive relationships and begin participating in loving relationships. We can heal from the years when nobody really cared about us by caring for ourselves and for others today. The following ideas may be helpful as we learn to live in a new land, free of abuse and neglect.

Safety First

If we want to heal from mistreatment, our personal safety comes first. Healing begins when we live in a place where we are free from the constant danger of further abuse or neglect. Most of us who are mistreated keep going back to our abuser with the hope that things will be better this time. We'll keep going back until we allow ourselves to feel the pain we are avoiding and fully understand the consequences of our choices both ourselves and our abusers.

Leaving destructive relationships behind is not giving up on the abuser or giving up hope. Leaving mistreatment is facing reality, looking toward a brighter future, and offering hope to our abusers and to us that we can both change and we can both heal.

Take Time

It takes time to heal—lots of time. There is no rigid timetable or set of requirements to pass off. Healing from a way of life that has become ingrained in our thought and behavior patterns takes gentle patience. It doesn't happen overnight. We should be as kind with ourselves as we would be to someone who is learning something new. It takes lots of practice to learn to value the new currency of healthy relationships. We've been deceived about the nature of love and need to relearn the value of this priceless means of exchange.

Feel Everything

We begin to heal from the effects of neglect by allowing ourselves to feel. Feelings are like an array of colorful crayons. There is not a right or wrong color or right or wrong feeling. We need all the colors to create a rainbow, and we need access to all our feelings to create our authentic selves. Unless we have access to all our emotions we are closing off essential avenues to healing. One of those emotions is sadness. It is a necessary part of healing to grieve for the relationship we wanted but will never have. We acknowledge and mourn our loss of trust, innocence, safety, or confidence. We allow ourselves to feel as bad as we really feel without embarrassment, self-consciousness, or shame.

If we allow ourselves to mourn, we will begin to see and understand the real and deeply personal effects of mistreatment in our lives. We will feel pain. We will face major life changes and a mountain of tears. We can choose not to feel or not to mourn, but we cannot escape by avoidance. Unmourned grief turns into depression. Depression is often bottled up anger without enthusiasm.

Look in the mirror and see you—really see you. Feel love for the child that was once you. Feel acceptance for the adult you are today. Allow yourself to cry. You didn't deserve to be abused or neglected and you can't go back and change what happened. Mourn for all that you longed for and never had. It is appropriate to grieve for the innocence and trust you have lost. Grief is gut-wrenching and painful but healing.

Don't keep returning to those who continue to abuse and neglect you. When someone intentionally harms you, it doesn't do any good to spend hours trying to convince them how much they hurt you. Those who abuse and neglect will always refuse to accept accountability for their words and actions because they live in a different reality. Stop waiting for them to see the error of their ways or ask for forgiveness. They are on their own journey. They won't change until they want to change.

Be patient with yourself as you begin your personal recovery process. Recovery takes time because it is really a two steps forward, one step back process. It is the direction you are headed that is important, not how fast you get there. Some of the wounds of neglect and abuse are deep and long lasting. The best way to heal is to be involved in a present relationship where you are treated with love, respect, and kindness. Before that happens, you may need to live alone for a season. When you respect yourself, being alone will not bother you. Each of us deserves to be safe at home.

Talk to Someone

We all need someone safe to talk to. It is most beneficial if that person will maintain eye contact, listen, and respond with compassion. This individual can be a trained counselor or a close friend. Talking to someone about our personal thoughts, worries, fears, and regrets allows us to let the jumble of anxiety in our heads find a safe place to land. Some people find that God is their best source for healing.

Seek support—don't isolate yourself. A natural instinct of many trauma survivors is to withdraw from others. That only makes things worse. Talk to a trusted friend or counselor. Join a support group. Individual psychotherapy can help you learn to love and care for yourself. Group therapy will help you feel less alone and more empathy for yourself and others.

Maintain Only Healthy Relationships

As we move along the path to healing, we will eventually understand that experiencing abuse and neglect has given us valuable experience that can teach us important lessons. If we learn from these lessons, we will not enter into another destructive relationship. We will learn ways to avoid or defend ourselves and others when we experience or witness mistreatment. Taking responsibility for our own actions and insisting others to do the same is the definition of maturity.

Nurture Self and Others

As we move still further along the journey of healing, we can learn to replace self-neglect with self-nurture. When we are mentally healthy and free of destructive relationships, we will find opportunities to teach and nurture others on their journey to healing. We can give others hope for a better life because we have a better life.

Make it a priority to get enough exercise, sleep, healthy food, meditation, and relaxation. Learn to look at yourself with compassion, patience, and tolerance. Forgive yourself for the mistakes you've made. Learn to love yourself in a deeper way. Think about all the good things about yourself. Treat your body and spirit with honor. Enjoy your senses. Find a new hobby. Remember that perfectionism is self-abuse. We want progress, not perfection. Perfection is not attainable. It leaves no room for small improvements, self-acceptance, or inner joy. You don't have to be perfect to be loved.

Move Toward Forgiveness

Most of us resist thinking about forgiveness because we think it has to happen right now. It takes as long as it takes to arrive at a point of forgiveness. Right now it is just fine to focus on moving in the direction toward forgiveness. Lots of things have to happen before we get there and we can be loving and patient with ourselves on that journey. Forgiveness is not accepting or condoning the behavior of those who mistreat us. Forgiveness is not about allowing abusive people to remain in our lives. Forgiveness is the way we remove ourselves from the devastating personal effects of abuse and neglect.

Feeling anger may be part of that journey. We can channel the anger we feel toward the abuser into the energy we need to be assertive and strong. When we are assertive and strong, we will not jump into another abusive relationship in the future. If left unacknowledged, anger controls us and causes internal rage or depression. If we remain consumed with anger, it is impossible to arrive at the inner place of peace and love. Holding on to anger is like drinking poison, believing it will hurt the abuser.

Everyone we come in contact with offers us gift. Those who treat us well give us happiness. Those who do not treat us well give us experience. Those who abuse and neglect offer us a valuable lesson. Some people come into our lives as a blessing and others as a lesson. It is wise to figure out what lesson an abuser is offering us before we allow them to destroy our soul and our hope for a better tomorrow.

Parents and partners who are neglectful, selfish, and abandoning do not necessarily set out to do these things. They are trapped in their own unfelt and unhealed pain. That pain has to go somewhere so they blame everyone around them for their destructive behavior. They are living in a state of unreality and refuse to take responsibility for the problems they create, the devastating effects of their destructive behavior, the consequences of their actions, and the heartwrenching agony they are causing others by their bad choices.

Ask for What You Want and Need

Those who have been mistreated have a difficult time articulating their own needs and wants. Many survivors of abuse have abdicated their personal rights and boundaries to the abuser for survival. Before long, we don't really know what we want or need. We don't feel we have the right to have a valid opinion on anything. We don't exist as people with our own hopes and dreams. We exist only to serve the demands of our abusers. Because we choose to maintain only healthy relationships, one day we can voice our opinions and know what we want. Someday we will stop trembling inside.

Change Old Habits Kindly and Gently

It would be nice if we could snap our fingers and all our old ways of surviving abuse and neglect could just disappear. Our unhealthy coping mechanisms don't magically change. It takes gentle self-analysis and time to see how we are behaving with any sense of objectivity. Changing personal habits begins one small step at a time. Sometimes we take one step forward and two steps back, but the direction we are heading matters most.

Let Nature Nurture

There is nothing like nature to renew and refresh our spirits. Every day we need to feel the wind on our face, walk through the trees, enjoy the sunrise and sunset, or listen to a wave crash on the shore. Our minds and hearts connect when we leave the stress of life and enjoy being part of the natural beauty all around us.

Create Something

There is something stimulating and energizing about the process of creation. It doesn't matter if we are creating a delicious meal, writing a poem, building a doll house, or designing a new home—creation is its own reward. In the process of creating we discover parts of ourselves that have been buried or forgotten. As we craft a new work, we are also re-creating our personal possibilities. Modern life often requires that we put our creative energies on hold while we earn a living. Prioritize your day to include time to make something with your own hands. Find your unique gift and create something that has not existed before.

Listen to Soothing Music as a Powerful Form of Prayer and Mediation

Music can soothe or energize the soul. When the effects of past destructive relationships weigh us down, beautiful music can bring us back up. Some things can only be understood with the heart. Music awakens our heart. Music frees us from the world of anxious and troubling thoughts and opens us to the world of freedom and feeling. Experience the joy of music like a child, before you had language to express yourself.

Write Down Your Story

Many people who have experienced abuse or neglect don't want to write about what happened to them. They have been keeping the secret for so long that they are afraid to think about it, let alone write it down. Writing it down makes it real. Many of us who have experienced abuse and neglect feel alone because we don't think we know anybody else who has been mistreated. Mistreatment is actually common even though nobody wants to talk about or share personal stories. When we share our story with others or write our story down, it frees us from the shame and guilt we have been carrying around for years. We make connections with others who have experienced similar life experiences.

Writing about our life is also useful self-therapy. In the process of writing, our brains help us to organize scattered anxious thoughts and feelings. When we take the time and emotional energy to write down our honest experiences and feelings, we have the opportunity to take an objective look at our life and deal more realistically with what is bothering us. When we keep things bottled up inside, we are less able to see the circumstances and people in our lives clearly. Consider writing a letter to yourself as a child or to your abuser to put some closure on your experience.

Discover the True Desires of Your Heart

All of us have deep inner yearnings. Most of us long for a loving family. Others desire to help humanity or perform a meaningful life's work. The way we discover the true desires of our heart is by creating restorative rhythms in our life that include work, rest, and recreation. Adults and children do better with a schedule. When we plan our day to include time for work and play, and meditation and creation we honor the rhythms of nature and life. There really is a time and a season for everything. It is easy to get out of balance. We are missing much of what gives life meaning if we don't give our bodies and minds work and rest. Relaxation and recreation are as important as we creation and productivity.

Find Daily Miracles

Look for and discover the miracles in everyday life. Each day we are alive is a grand thing. Our physical bodies are magnificent. The ability to see, hear, touch, feel, and think is a miracle. Look into the eyes of a child with greater tenderness. Meditate as you wash the dishes. Find your sweetheart and dance in the moonlight before you go to bed. The present moment is your finest gift. Receive it with thanksgiving.

Focus on the Abundance in Life—Not What Is Missing

We all have much more good in our life than bad. Destructive relationships in the past don't have to prevent us from having a full, rich, and meaningful life today. After we heal from abuse and neglect, we are smarter, stronger, and wiser. When we count our blessings instead of our misfortunes, we will be more likely to notice all that is right with our lives.

Become Genuinely Interested in Others.

An important part of the healing process comes when we look outward and help those around us. It is difficult to become whole and healthy if we remain focused only on our own pain. Thinking about the needs of others frees our spirit from the chains we've known.

Don't rush your encounters with people. Take time to know and love them.

Many of us are too busy to relish and enjoy our encounters with other people. When we take a moment to really look into the eyes and heart of the person we are talking to, we will see that those around us are starved for attention and love. Take the time to listen and understand. When we reach out to others with genuine interest, they sense our caring and respond with increased honesty and spontaneity. Notice what is right with those around you. Though it may be more difficult to trust people after we have been rejected, abandoned, or neglected, we will discover that many people out there make great friends and acquaintances.

Make It a Priority to Bless the Lives of Those Closest to You

We don't have to wait for our lives to be perfect before we can bless the lives of those around us. The cashier needs a kind word as well as the person who delivers our mail. We feel better when we allow someone to cut in front of us on the freeway without getting upset. Reach out to your neighbors who need your smile or attention. Stop waiting for others to appreciate you and start appreciating them.

Reframe Your Idea of Wealth

See value in people, not possessions. We are rich when we are surrounded by people we love and are loved by. Just because we have been mistreated in the past doesn't mean we need to give up on the human race. Many wonderful people out there are willing to practice the art of love with us. If we stay on this journey to healing wholeness and don't give up, we will eventually find people who value our love. Because of our past experience, we will value the love offered to us with deeper appreciation.

No matter how many material possessions we acquire, we won't find real joy until people mean more to us than property. We are stewards, not owners. Everything we own is only ours for a few short years and then we die. The guy with the most belongings when he dies doesn't win; the guy who wins is the one who blesses the most lives. Our lives have more meaning when we use everything we have, including our time, talents, and money to bless the lives of as many people as possible. True wealth resides in loving relationships.

Live in the Moment

Learning to be compassionate to ourselves every day helps us heal from neglect. One way to do this is by developing the ability to focus on the feelings and sensations we are having at any given moment during the day. Ask yourself, "How am I feeling right now? Am I hungry? Am I tired? Do I feel lonely? Then we can take quick action. We eat something nourishing, find a friend to talk to, or give ourselves time to rest. Behavior problems are often misguided attempts to meet legitimate unmet needs. We can become aware of our needs and fill them in life-enhancing ways before we result to unhealthy addictions or behaviors.

Create a New Life Plan

Have a life plan. Write it down and be specific. Keep a journal and document your progress. Take parenting and marriage classes. Check for social service resources at your local school, church, or mental health agency. Look for someone to be your friend who is happily married or widowed. Learn from them or use them as a role model. Learn to let go of people and circumstances that prevent your growth and development. No longer allow bad memories to rule your life. Practice saying self-affirming statements such as the following:

- I am a good enough person.
- I refuse to trash myself.
- I will not examine details over and over.
- I will not try to control the uncontrollable.
- I will not jump to conclusions.
- I will not endlessly second-guess myself.
- I forgive all my past mistakes.
- I can't make the future perfectly safe.
- I will stop hunting for what could go wrong.

UNHEALTHY DEPENDENCY

Each person in a relationship needs the ability to express his or her rights, needs, and boundaries. Neglect causes a disorder of assertiveness that causes a person to attract and accept exploitation, abuse, and neglect. This learned helplessness began when we were children. It is important to remember that we are not helpless now. We have the right to express our rights, needs, and personal boundaries. We are not at the mercy of those who harm us.

As children we learned that in order to be safe we had to become useful to our parents. Servitude, ingratiation, and forfeiture of any needs that might inconvenience or ire our parents was the only survival strategy available to us. Many of us surrendered our normal healthy boundaries to appease our caregivers. Our parents chose not to change and become loving people who were there for us. They never grew up and became adults willing to sacrifice for the well-being of their children. So we became as useful to our dysfunctional parent as possible by performing such roles like housekeeper, confidante, lover, sounding board, or surrogate parent for other siblings.

This loss of self profoundly affects all future relationships if we are not aware of it. Every human being is precious and has the right to express her own personality, needs, and wants. When we are not aware of our loss of self, we continue this servile behavior whenever we run into someone who mistreats us. We easily abdicate our rights and needs to appease the abuser. Our partner's or parent's betrayal and neglect eventually turns into self-betrayal and neglect. It is healing when we allow ourselves to feel disappointed and sickened at the image of our caregivers or partners bullying us and overwhelming us with the shame and guilt they refused to feel, especially when we were defenseless children.

The following sentences give voice to breaking unhealthy bonds to parents or partners.

- "I'm not afraid of you."
- "I won't allow you to hurt me anymore."

- "I am handing back the shame and guilt you refused to feel."
- "I will not let the critics of my life win by joining or agreeing with them."
- "I no longer neglect myself."
- "I care for myself."
- "I respect myself."
- "I feel afraid, but that will not stop me from doing what is right."
- "I am not in trouble when I stand up for myself."
- "I will not paralyze myself with fearful thoughts about what my abusers will do to me."
- "I don't need to rush or hurry. I enjoy my life at a relaxed pace."
- "I no longer accept unfair criticism or perfectionistic expectations."
- "I expect those I associate with to treat me with kindness and respect."
- "I have legal authorities to defend me if threatened by those who want to hurt me."

HEALING A PARENT/PARTNER WOUND

One way to heal a parent or partner wound is to find another person who can serve as a role model. Most people repeat their parents' behavior. If we don't like our parents' behavior, we can follow the example of a loving parental role model and allow them to mentor us. Older people can make wonderful friends and teachers. Look for someone who has built a loving marriage and family. They have some marvelous secrets to share.

Young children are also great teachers who love freely and

forgive quickly. We all had these qualities as children but most of us have forgotten ourselves. Telling our story to someone who has compassion for us can be incredibly validating and healing. Look for friends who have compassion by becoming a compassionate person. We know we are on the road to healing when we like ourselves and have the ability to fill our lives with activities and people who bring us enjoyment, peace, and joy. It is possible to surround ourselves with people who we like and who like us back. It is possible to surround ourselves with people who we love and people who love us back.

Now What?

If we have experienced mistreatment we need to accept, understand, decide, and begin.

First, we need to accept the reality that we have been neglected. It often takes years before we finally face this personal painful reality. Continuing to live with mistreatment is the perfect breeding ground for developing a mental disorder. We don't have to be embarrassed about mental health issues. Mental disorders don't have to be permanent. With a lot of time and persistence, we can reorder our thought process and rewire our brain.

Second, we need to understand that enduring an abusive relationship is not a virtue. Remaining in relationships where we are being abused and neglected hurts us *and* the abuser. When we draw a line in the sand, we can access multiple resources to help us. Numerous self-help books, counselors, support groups, and community and church programs are available.

Third, we need to decide what we are going to do about our situation. The person who abuses or neglects us may have a reason for their behavior, but this reason is not an excuse. Since we control no one but ourselves, we need to determine if our situation is likely to change. If our circumstances are not likely to change, we need to accept that staying is hurting everyone. Because both we and our children live with the consequences of this decision, drawing on professional or ecclesiastical help to assist us in making this important decision may be useful.

Fourth, we begin a journey to healing. If we can feel, we can heal. Healing from destructive relationships is an extensive journey of self-discovery. After we leave neglectful relationships we soon discover than we are in a habit of neglecting ourselves. It takes time and patient effort to keep the healing process going.

At some point along the road to healing, we will discover that we are at peace. Accepting what happened does not mean we condone it. Accepting means we understand that we can't change the past, only our response to it. Forgiveness is not really forgetting what happened but the ability to remember with peace. Difficult life experiences give us painful yet meaningful knowledge, and we become stronger people for it.

Like the characters in the classic tale of the tortoise and the hare, it is not always the swiftest that wins the race. Healing is a slow process that may take a lifetime. But if we keep moving toward the finish line, we will eventually get there. The naysayers and those who try to convince us that we are inadequate are quite simply wrong. We are enough just as we are. Our personal race is always lined with those who try to trip us up and those who cheer us on. Listen to the ones who cheer. See yourself moving, though slowly at times, toward a better life filled with love. The person with the most love in their heart is the one who wins the race of life.

Questions to Answer

We eventually realize it is not mentally, physically, or emotionally healthy for us to remain in a relationship with someone who abuses or neglects us. If we continue to live in a destructive relationship after we know better, we must also take responsibility for the damaging results this decision creates in the life of our abuser, ourselves, our children, and our community. If we stay, no one changes and no one heals. If we stay, we don't model what it means to truly love and be loved for the next generation.

Those who come after us need us to be mentally healthy role models and show them what it means to be a loving, caring adult. If we ignore or minimize our destructive relationship and refuse to be that model, how will the next generation learn? The following are some questions to consider when we are making the decision to hold our abuser accountable.

- Am I an example of a strong, caring person for those around me?
- Have I considered how my choice to stay in an abusive or neglectful relationship is going to effect the next generation?
- If I stay in this destructive relationship, what will happen in the future?
- Do I understand that I deserve to be treated with kindness and respect?
- Am I a harsh judge of myself?

- Do I often feel afraid?
- Do I often have negative thoughts about myself?
- How do I resolve conflict?
- Does my partner or parent lose his temper often?
- How do my parents treat each other?
- Am I afraid of my partner or parent?
- How does my partner or parents make me feel when we are alone?
- Do I try to look good to others when I am hurting inside?
- Do I understand that the patriarchal order is not an excuse to abuse or neglect?
- Do I believe in and encourage blind obedience because of my religious beliefs?
- Do I believe that suffering and pain are essential elements of this life and that I should tolerate destructive relationships for some reward in the afterlife?
- Do I have the skills to cope with the pressures of adult life?
- What steps do I need to take in order to begin the healing process?
- Where can I find help to leave a marriage or family where I am abused and neglected?
- How do I let go of fear and learn to love?
- How can I find joy and peace in my life?
- How are my decisions going to affect my children?
- Why do I tolerate abuse and neglect?
- Where do I draw the line between casual indifference and abusive neglect?

Section Four
Rewriting Neglect

Chapter Seven

THE ROLE OF FAITH

Our personal belief system is an important part of how we cope with neglect and abuse. The link between spirituality and mental health is multifaceted and important to understand because it is vital to our well-being. A large body of research shows that religiously devout people in any denomination enjoy positive mental health benefits and improved psychological adjustment to the difficulties of life. Multiple studies support the idea that being involved in religion is beneficial to our mental health.

The way we actually *live* our faith determines how our beliefs affect our mental health. Simply put, knowing and believing must evolve into how we conduct ourselves every day. In other words, the way we internalize our belief system is what actually affects our well-being. If we hold a certain set of beliefs and then don't live up to those values and standards of conduct, we are more likely to have poor mental health. If we actually follow the doctrines we espouse to believe and are involved in a religious community, our mental health improves. This positive result comes only if our motivation is pure.

If we go to religious services because it is socially acceptable, we don't want to be judged, or because we want to have more contacts for business, it will actually cause mental health issues, not help them. If we use our faith as an excuse to passively accept our personal problems and do nothing to solve them, then we are using our religion as a crutch. Our faith or set of values and standards of personal behavior should help us chart a course to achieve positive personal change. All faiths teach self-improvement and greater responsibility to care for the needs of others. But some of us use our faith as an excuse to harm others. For example, some of us deny responsibility for what we have done and refuse to be accountable for how our actions have impacted others' lives.

Some of us use our religious beliefs to stereotype other people of faith and are too quick to cast blame on the entire religious community of followers for the actions of a select few of their misguided members. Every religious faith has its fair share of people who are mentally unstable and who act irresponsibly. When we respect the differences and beliefs of all men and women, we can add new insights to our core beliefs and expand our ability to find truth in multiple sources. We are also less likely to use our own religion as an excuse not to respond to any form of human cruelty, even if that cruelty is coming from the people in our own homes and families.

Another example of how religious faith can be used unconstructively is when we blame a supreme being for our problems. If we believe that God orchestrates the events in our lives to curse us, we are more likely to suffer with poor mental health. Also, our faith doesn't give us the right to control the choices of others. Some of us use our positions of leadership in a religious community to exercise unrighteous dominion. We believe we have the right to tell others what to do and condemn all who don't do what we think is best.

We all have our fair share of difficulties. Challenges are common to all of us. How we respond to the difficulties of life is the way we grow and change for the better or regress and stifle our potential. If we use our faith to motivate us to meditate, consider the meaning and purpose of life, and to pray, our mental health will be improved. When we are mentally healthy, we are less likely to stay in destructive relationships for any reason.

On the other hand, devout people are not immune to mental health issues. Many psychological issues are biological or genetic. Just because we are living a good life, it doesn't follow that we won't have multiple problems to face. Those of us who misunderstand the positive role of religious faith can be confused and come to believe that the bad things that happen to us are because we did something wrong and we're being punished. Of course, some of the hard things that happen to us are the direct result of our behavior, but the vast majority of difficulties we face happen to us by no fault of our own.

Life is hard. Once we accept the reality that life is difficult, we are free to focus on the here and now instead of wallowing in regrets from the past or debilitating fear of the future. We will have better mental health if we understand that where we stand today and the direction we are headed is more important than what happened yesterday. We can move forward with hope at any moment in time. On the other hand, if we use our religion as an excuse to be overly judgmental of ourselves or those around us, our misunderstanding of our faith is harming us. Using our core values as an excuse to cast final judgment or eternal condemnation on ourselves and others is never a productive way to live and learn.

If our core system of belief is helping us learn how to love ourselves and others, then our belief system is helping us. Standards of conduct can help us determine if our behavior is loving or unloving, but it shouldn't move us to condemn or curse others. If we use our faith as the reason we believe that we'll never be good enough, our mental health suffers. If we feel constantly unworthy and broken beyond repair, then our belief system is holding us back from healing. If we use religion to develop self-defeating attitudes then we need to reevaluate our interpretation of our faith. We change our behavior and make our life better when we feel loved and accepted, not cursed and degraded.

One way religion promotes good mental health is by providing a social network where we have a group of friends of like faith to help us in times of need. A religious community can also be a source of great strength during times of difficulty. An arm around the shoulder, personal visit, a warm meal, or a kind word from those in our congregation can prove to be a lifeline at difficult times. It doesn't matter if we are the person who is offering the love and care or accepting it, a community of faithful believers can be the anchor in the storm of life.

Some of us use religion as a reason not to seek help in the professional community when we are struggling with abuse and neglect. Some feel that we just need to increase our faith or be more righteous and all our problems would disappear. It is important to realize that professional help and medication can be great assets as we face the inevitable difficulties of life. There was a time when leprosy was treated with isolation and fear because of lack of knowledge. We don't need to treat mental health issues similarly today. If we don't take advantage of all the resources available to us, then we limit our ability to heal. Our system of belief should help us move forward in life with hope and courage. Our faith should invite us to learn and practice the art of loving and be loved.

As I have previously stated, one of the ways we cope with destructive relationships is by stifling our emotions. We push our difficult thoughts and emotions into the back of our minds where we don't have to think about them or deal with them. We choose not to deal with our abusive relationships. The problem with that coping mechanism is that this choice has serious consequences for both our mental and physical health. Facing stressful situations with a plan is always healthier than ignoring or pretending they don't exist. Examples of physical reactions to repressed emotions are gastric upsets, chest pain, body aches, hives, and a wide assortment of other indicators. This is the way our body tells us that something is wrong and needs our attention.

As we discussed earlier, destructive relationships activate cortisol and other stress hormones that disrupt many body processes. This over-supply of hormones can trigger physical problems that add to our mental health issues. A great body of research suggests that long-term and unresolved stress can increase our risk of heart disease, sleep problems, digestive issues, depression, obesity, mental impairment, a wide assortment of skin conditions, and multiple other physical conditions. The mind and body connection is real and powerful.

We all face stressful situations every day. Our faith should help us believe that hope and change are always possible. We need to know deep down that we can surmount our problems with faith, courage, and lots of elbow grease. We need inner strength and competence to accomplish whatever task is required of us. We need the absolute conviction that we are not victims to be tossed to and fro by our circumstances and those who harm us. We need to know that we are strong, able, and competent enough to rise above the cruel people and disappointing circumstances that hold us back from becoming the magnificent people we already are. If our core beliefs help us to access all these inner strengths, then our faith is an aid to our mental health and stability.

There are ways to cope with stress that promote both mental and physical health. There are coping mechanisms that can be practiced or improved. It helps to ask, "Does my religious faith promote helpful coping mechanisms for the inevitable stress of life?" The following are some ideas to consider.

Know Your Limits

Sometimes we have a difficult time recognizing just how much stress we can handle. We have a hard time saying no and put too much on our plates. Saying no to one more thing to do is saying yes to improved mental and physical health. Many of us remain victims because we lack the ability to say no to those who control, manipulate, or harm us.

Meet Your Own Self-Care Needs First

Most of us who have been abused and neglected, put our needs last. If we are not eating a nutritious diet, getting a proper amount of sleep and engaging in regular exercise, our mental and physical health will suffer. It is unselfish to take good care of ourselves because a healthy person has the energy and health to be a force for good.

Learn How to Manage Your Time Efficiently

If we are in a destructive relationship, the only time-management tool we use is keeping the peace at any price. We start believing that our time is not our own. Every minute of every day is at the beck and call of those who control or manipulate us. There is a difference between being helpful to those around us and being subservient to the point of self-neglect. Our time and our love is our most precious gift.

Examine Expectations for Yourself

Many of us in destructive relationships demand perfection from ourselves. We use any displeasure expressed by our abusive parent or partner as proof that we will never be good enough. If our efforts are less than stellar, we beat up ourselves and add to our stress. It is time to remove ourselves from abusive relationships and reexamine our overly perfectionistic expectations.

Accept What You Can't Change

Many of us who have been abused and neglected like to hold out hope that the person we love will eventually love us back. We refuse to accept that an abusive partner or parent will not love us back. We keep ourselves in a stressful situation by refusing to face the facts and deal with the reality of our life. We can't change our abuser. We can only change ourselves.

Do What Needs to Be Done, Now

We usually put off doing what causes us the most stress. Yet the decision not to act causes us even more stress. If we are in a destructive relationship, we must remove ourselves and create a safe and loving home. The first step is always the hardest to take. Inaction becomes a habit. Refusing to tolerate of abuse and neglect may cause some stress right now, but the stress will diminish as we place ourselves in safe places.

Create a Peaceful, Loving Environment

When we live in a safe place free from abuse and neglect, we can begin creating an authentic life in which we can learn to love and be loved. It doesn't matter if we need to live alone for a season. Many things are worse than being alone. Living with someone who does not treat you with kindness and respect is a living hell.

Simplify

Simplify your life. Don't take on more than you can reasonably accomplish and still leave time for rest and restoration. Life is stressful. We don't need to complicate matters even more by taking on more responsibilities than we can manage. One of the best ways to simplify is to ask for help. Many people who have been abused and neglected believe they are alone and must face life without help. The ability to ask for help when we need it is actually a sign of strength, not weakness.

Live in the Present

Much of our stress is caused by living with regrets from the past or fear of the future. We wallow in remorse or live in dread of what might happen. Choosing to live in the moment is choosing to experience the reality of today and use our power to act now. We let go of regrets and fear when we understand that all power resides in the moment. What we do right now is the most important. The past and the future only reside in our minds. This moment is the time to act. All present moments line up to constitute the reality of our life. When we replace negative and fearful thoughts with positive loving thoughts, our here and now becomes a little piece of personal paradise.

See the Beauty Inside

After we have removed ourselves from a destructive relationship, we have the tendency to get into a new one because we haven't changed the way we see ourselves. We have the responsibility to self-nurture and place ourselves in positive situations surrounded by people who are capable of treating us with kindness and respect. We have the duty to look inside our hearts and find the exquisite person inside.

Create a Positive Community Support System

If we are in a destructive relationship, the tendency is to retreat from our extended families, neighborhood, community, or religious group when we need them the most. We all need the helpful and objective eyes and hands of others who help us see how to remove ourselves from the disrespect we are experiencing at home. Government agencies, church leaders and members, and professionals stand by ready to offer assistance.

Prepare for Change

When we are involved in abusive and neglectful relationships, change is absolutely required. It helps to prepare ourselves for that change, one step at a time and not wait for a moment of crisis to make life-changing changes. We prepare for change financially, emotionally, physically, and spiritually. We also prepare for change by amassing an army of professionals or a loving support group that will stand by us when we need the resolve to stick with our decision. If necessary, we can stand alone.

Get Counseling and Take Medication if Necessary

Shop for a counselor who you can trust and who puts you at ease. If you don't like one you've tried, try another until you find a good fit. If a health care professional recommends medication, take it. Some of us do not have brains that produce the right amount of certain chemicals. We may need these chemicals to function normally. It is a sign of strength to address our issues so we don't harm others by self-neglect.

Change the Situation

Make a firm decision to maintain only healthy relationships. When we take the first step to change, the one that scares us most, the rest of the journey is easier. That first step is always the most difficult. Stand up for what is right even if you have to stand alone for a season.

Healing from a Relationship We Didn't End

The person who is abusive or neglectful is often the one who ends a relationship. In other words: we don't leave them; they leave us. Many of us have experienced what it feels like when those we care deeply about simply walk away and never look back. Whether this happens to us as children or as adults, the pain is profound. We often conclude that we are defective, not good enough, and not important. In truth, the person who leaves is dealing with difficult personal issues that have nothing to do with us. Until those issues are dealt with and resolved, they are closed off or blind to the needs of those closest to them. Yet others' choices can only hinder our progress if we allow them. When those we love don't love us, it is because they are incapable of returning our love at this point in their journey.

Those we love can walk away from us physically or emotionally. Physical and emotional abandonment can be harder to get over than death. With death, at least the person who died didn't *want* to leave us. When we love someone and they choose not to love us back and, in fact, reject, abuse, and neglect us, it is easy to blame ourselves. We rack our minds and hearts for something we did wrong or a reason why. When we hang onto this self-blame, we keep the destructive behavior going with self-abuse and neglect.

On the other hand, we may respond to abandonment with anger and bitterness toward the person who rejected us. This response allows the person who neglected us great power over our present peace of mind and ability to heal and move forward. While all emotions must be felt and dealt with, if we stay stuck in anger or bitterness, we won't attract others to us who are kind and respectful. We will attract others who are stuck in anger and bitterness. Two people stuck in negative emotions will not have a happy life together. If we stay stuck there, we continue to give the person who abused and neglected us great power over us. We can't quit thinking of our abusers and feeling the hurt. We can't quit living our present lives as a direct response to the past. After we move through the healing process, we can let the abuse go in love and peace.

When we blame ourselves for the behavior of someone else, we say in effect,

- "You certainly made a good choice when you chose to abandon and reject me.
- "I'm not worth any sacrifice."
- "I am unlovable, and you were right to leave."
- "I'm not important."
- "I'm not worthy of your love and acceptance."
- "There is something very wrong with me."
- "I'm not worthy of love."
- "Why should anyone care about me?"
- "I'm defective."
- "I don't know why you didn't leave me sooner."
- "I would leave me too."

Of course, we cover up these thoughts with sadness, anger, or resentment, but the effects of this thinking lives on inside us with lingering internal doubts. It is difficult to ask this question and find a satisfactory answer, but it is possible.

"If I am worthy of love, why doesn't the person I love, love me back?"

The answer is, they don't know how to love us and they don't want to learn right now. They are so damaged from the lack of love they experienced that they can't see that they are doing the same thing to us.

All of us are worthy of love. It is difficult to feel worthy of love when the person we choose to love does not love us back, but it is entirely possible. If we have no experience with being loved, we usually have a hard time knowing how to love—especially ourselves. Just because we chose to love people incapable of loving us back doesn't mean we are stupid. We are merely students of love, and we learn important truths from all our relationships. Real love is a choice, not just a feeling. Our feelings are as fleeting as the wind. A choice, on the other hand, involves a commitment and the determination to see this through, even in hard times.

The people we love can also leave us emotionally. They may physically stay and live with us, but their love and loyalty is marginalized by affairs, addictions, abuse, and neglect. We are not a priority in their life. Many of us stay in relationships because we are afraid of the unknown, or we're trapped because we are children. We have confused loyalties. One woman told me about the effects of neglect in her family:

> My mother physically, emotionally, and sexually abused me and my siblings. When I told my father, he did nothing. His neglect destroyed our family just as much as my mother's abuse. My father held many high-level church leadership responsibilities, and he didn't want anyone to know that there was trouble at home. He was good at putting on a public face and pretending everything was all right.
>
> He dealt with the trouble in his family by avoiding home whenever possible. But he kept getting mom pregnant. She couldn't deal with the stress of a large family, and I was required to take over the household chores and babysitting. Year after year, Mom got worse and worse. We all struggled to deal with my parents' dysfunctional marriage. Mom and Dad would yell and scream at each other for hours in their bedroom and come out bruised and scratched.
>
> Some of us denied what was going on; others acted out with addictions and obsessive-compulsive behavior. When it came time for us to choose partners, we each either became an abuser or married one—or we neglected ourselves or our own children. As the years went by, I watched my siblings deteriorate mentally. I watched the effect of their dysfunctional marriages

on my nieces and nephews and one divorce after another.

I asked my father once, "Why didn't you protect us from Mom? Why did you always take Mom's side?"

He replied emphatically, "Because that is what I thought a good husband was supposed to do!"

I followed his answer with this, "What did you think a good father was supposed to do?"

He didn't answer me.

Now I know that neglect is just as destructive as abuse. What you don't do can be as destructive as what you do. I think my mother was bipolar and in desperate need of counseling and medication. That never happened. I've also come to believe that she was abused as a child. I see and feel the long-term multigenerational results of abuse and neglect in my family every single day. The total breakdown of my extended family is a tragedy that didn't have to happen."

The Need to Be Loved

We were born to be loved. When we are denied love or we deny others love, we live a narrow life that leads to emptiness and despair. Only by lasting and loving human connections do we find meaning and purpose to life. Love is the answer to all life's most difficult issues. We don't need to live in quiet desperation, searching for something that will not satisfy. There is no substitute for love. There is no other remedy for the difficulties and struggles of life.

Neglect is the big lie that says:

"I don't matter."

"You don't matter."

The truth is, you and I are worth the effort of human caring, the dignity of respect, and the obligation of duty. We all deserve to experience the joy of creating lasting and loving relationships. Each of us does matter. The greatest abuse of power is the refusal to love those who have given us their hearts. As we more clearly see the good and the bad, the black and the white, the loving and the unloving, we are better able to rewrite our stories.

Life is so fleeting. Choosing to spend the precious time allotted to us living with those who do not love us is life's greatest tragedy. The more rejected, abandoned, and abused we are, the greater need we have to love, champion, and respect ourselves. No one can diminish us without our permission. When we allow others to abuse and neglect us, we do not become more forgiving or more loving. Enabling cruel behavior doesn't serve anyone.

And so . . . "Cinderella stayed with her stepmother and sisters all her life and died abused and rejected because she didn't believe she deserved anything better" will *not* be the way our story ends.

Chapter Eight

REWARDING NEGLECT

One of the greatest tragedies occurs when we *choose* to remain our stories as victims. We all encounter trials, but remaining in an abusive relationship after we know better does not just happen to us; we choose this disaster. We choose to remain a target. We reward those who abuse and neglect us by staying where they put us. Someone can victimize us without our consent, but they can't make us stay their prey forever. Abusers may have controlled part of our lives, but we own the rest. When we decide to change from abuse victims to thriving survivors, we reward ourselves with inner courage, self-respect, dignity, and peace of mind.

We always have the opportunity to change our circumstances. No matter what has happened to us, no matter how bad we feel, we need to get up and fight for our lives. When someone mistreats us, we can't let the mistreatment continue without damaging our souls. When we do nothing, we also harm those who come after us. Abuse and neglect not only affect us, they change the course of events in the lives of our posterity.

The Effects of Neglect on Families

We often read about the adverse effects of divorce on children. We don't read much about the adverse effects on children when their parents stay in a loveless marriage. Though divorce should be avoided if possible, no one should advise someone to stay in a marriage where they are abused and neglected. Children learn what they see and experience. The relationship we have with our partner will soon become the relationship our child has with their partner. And so the tragic circle continues for another generation. The truth is, when people stay in an abusive marriage, it always hurts everybody. One woman described her life story this way:

> My ex-husband wasn't honest with me before we married. He pretended to be someone he wasn't. After a year, I wanted out. I should have left right then, but I stayed. I really didn't think I could do any better or that anyone else would want me. I adopted a baby from the foster care system to fill in the empty hole. But the baby was demanding and had learning difficulties. My ex wasn't a good provider, so I had to go work. My son was left alone for long hours at home without adult supervision. He got into pornography and drugs as a teenager and began lying to me about his other bad choices. I finally kicked him out, but my husband said if our son had to leave, he would go with him. So I said good riddance to both of them. I live alone now. I'm too old and fat to find anyone else. I wish I'd done something sooner. I shouldn't have ruined the life of that boy who could have gone to a loving home.

One woman told me about her grandmother's decision to stay in an abusive marriage with a husband who had multiple affairs. After this grandmother's husband died, she turned to her daughter and said, "I've been waiting for your father to tell me that he loved me my whole life, but he never did."

This grandmother did not believe that she and her children could survive financially without her husband to provide for them. She chose to stay. She chose to continue being abused and neglected. What this woman didn't know was that she was beginning a multigenerational family pattern. She became the model for her daughters and granddaughters who followed her. Because her posterity loved her, they chose to see their grandmother's victimhood as acceptable and perhaps even virtuous. Yet this choice to stay tragically played out in the lives of her posterity.

Years later, her granddaughter began dating a man she thought was wonderful. She soon learned differently as he became physically, emotionally, and sexually abusive. Following a family pattern, she chose to stay in the relationship even though she was tortured and eventually raped. Her parents sent her away to live with strangers and refused to talk about it when they found out she was pregnant. She gave up her infant son for adoption. What she didn't realize at the time was that the medical personal had botched her C-section and rendered her unable to have any more children. Though she eventually left her abusive boyfriend, the effects of that destructive relationship played out in her later choice of a husband.

> I dated a "safe" man for two and a half years before we got married. He was everything my first boyfriend wasn't. There was no more abuse or no forced physical intimacy. I felt safe. His parents pushed for the marriage, and I went along. After we got married, my new husband never wanted to be intimate. I had to initiate every time. After three years, he moved out of our bedroom, and we've never been intimate since. We've been married for twenty-two years now.

This granddaughter chose to stay in a demeaning and torturous dating relationship even though she was horribly abused. Today she chooses to stay in a marriage where she is gravely neglected. While we all must accept responsibility for our personal choices, we also have to consider that we are models for those around us. While it is obvious that this woman's grandfather chose to neglect his wife, it is not so obvious that her grandmother also neglected herself and her posterity.

I'm sure this grandmother was a good woman who didn't realize that her choice to stay in a destructive relationship would affect future generations, but it did. While it is never advisable to judge past generations with the insight and knowledge we have today, it is advisable to learn from them and try to do better. Are we sending the message that it is all right for our parent or partner to abuse or neglect us? Choosing to stay in a destructive relationship hurts everyone involved. Choosing to remain a victim always hurts and never heals. If we want to stop the plague of abuse and neglect, we need to see a way out and a way up.

Tolerating Neglect

Information about the multigenerational harm caused from abusive or neglectful relationships won't make any difference until we as victims change the way we feel about ourselves. Even if we leave one destructive relationship, we quickly jump into another. Though it is hard to admit this to ourselves, some of us get something out of our victimhood. We have to ask ourselves if staying in an abusive relationship is fulfilling some mistaken or unconscious need. It is fine to occasionally make sacrifices for someone we love but if we sacrifice ourselves *all the time* because that is how we get our sense of worth, we are doing it for the wrong reason. If we sacrifice all the time because we desperately need the other person's approval, we are doing it for ourselves, not that person. This behavior is a problem because we are behaving in a sacrificial way to get what we need—approval and a sense of worth—not because our sacrifice is what the other person needs.

Some of us stay in relationships where we are mistreated because we have a sad story to tell, and we get sympathy and attention from others. Staying gives us a built-in excuse not to succeed or to make bad choices. Staying gives us someone else to blame for all our problems and failures. There are hundreds of ill-advised reasons or excuses for staying in destructive relationships. All of these reasons and excuses lead to multigenerational stagnation, disaster, and tragic conclusions. Some of us stay because we care too much about what others will think. Others stay because we don't see our way out financially or we don't want to break up the family. Still others stay because they don't want to hurt their reputations or believe that choice is better for the children.

It is important to remember that sometimes the most loving behavior does not appear to be nice. Sometimes we have to tell people things they don't want to hear. Sometimes we have to do things that will not make the other person happy. Sometimes we must choose to love ourselves and do what is right for us because we are just as important as the other person. There are times when we have to tell the other person things they don't want to hear because it is the truth and they need to hear it. Healthy relationships require a give-and-take balance; it takes wisdom to know when to give and when to receive.

One of the biggest reasons some of us tolerate neglect is that we feel responsible for the problems and feelings of other people, especially members of our family. In truth, we are not responsible for other people's problems and feelings. We can care about others and be supportive as they work through their feelings and problems, but we are not responsible for them—they are. On the other hand, we have the responsibility to discontinue our attempts to be supportive when we are being mistreated. We don't have to have someone's approval to feel good about ourselves. We can be confident, strong, and independent without the approval of those we love. There is nothing wrong with wanting someone to love, but when we feel we are not complete unless we are in a relationship with another person—no matter how that person treats us—we will maintain associations that are not good for either person.

Most of us are driven by the fear that we are not good enough. We are afraid of being abandoned. We don't realize that we each are the only person we will never lose or leave. For that reason, we need to be our own best friends. We don't have to spend our whole lives seeking approval from others or waste our precious time adding to our list of accomplishments, trying to feel validated. Other people can never adequately fill our empty well; we must fill it ourselves. We gain a sense of strength and confidence when we love others but also when we love ourselves. We need others, but we don't need others to feel complete.

If we feel fulfilled by giving too much, people who give too little will find us. Those who mistreat others are attracted to people who are insecure or fearful about their own value. They know on some level that we do nice things for people because that is how we feel our sense of importance. Those who mistreat others see us as weak and easy to manipulate. They do not respect us. Until we feel our own value to the core and refuse to be manipulated, we will not respect ourselves. Until we respect ourselves, we will never receive respect from others.

We are not responsible to make other people happy or solve their problems. Those who mistreat us will constantly try to convince us that we are responsible for them in loud and dramatic ways. They will tell us over and over that we are responsible to make them happy and solve their problems. We are not. They are responsible for their own happiness, and they must solve their own problems. In every relationship, we must clearly see what we do and do not control. We must learn what we are and are not responsible for. The people in our lives are responsible for *their* problems, choices, and feelings; we are responsible for *ours*. We can love people, but we can't fix them. We need to work on our own feelings of self-worth first so that we can stop enabling mistreatment from those around us.

We should not tolerate disrespect and mistreatment in any form for any reason. Abuse is not acceptable. We must not allow others to neglect, abandon, ignore, threaten, control, demean, or lie to us. Each of us deserves to be treated with kindness. We deserve to be listened to and have our opinions validated. Our thoughts and feelings are important. Even when others do not agree with our opinions, we still deserve to have a voice. When others express their opinions, they must do it in a way that doesn't harm, negate, or belittle us.

We must learn to deal with relationships issues as strong, confident, and mature adults. When others treat us without respect, we must understand that nothing others think, feel, or express can diminish who we are. Our value as human beings is infinite and absolute. Our value remains constant. No one takes our power away from us, and no one continues to hurt us without our consent. When we feel our own value and worth to the core of our soul, we will handle our relationships with more confidence and self-respect. We will deal with difficult relationship issues with less emotion and fear.

When others demand that we engage in conflict with them, we have the right to physically remove ourselves for our own safety. We do not have to engage in any conversation unless we are spoken to with respect. We must insist that others show us respect and refuse to deal with them until they do. When we value ourselves and insist on being treated with respect and kindness, we may discover that some people will treat us differently. Others will continue their destructive behavior. We take away the opportunity others have to harm us when we remove ourselves from destructive relationships. Once we leave our "I'm-not-good-enough" fears behind, we walk out of a fog and into the clear day. Then we see ourselves and others more clearly. Then we will attract completely different people. Our future relationships will be better.

One of the most important lessons we learn is to separate *who* we are from *where* we are on our life's journey. We can choose to see everything that happens to us as a learning opportunity. Our value, or who we are, remains constant no matter what happens to us or what choices we have made. We can lose many things, such as our money, reputation, and friends, but we can't lose or leave ourselves or our value. Our mistakes don't change who we are. Lots of good people make bad choices. Even when we make really bad mistakes, that does not change who we are. As long as we keep learning and growing we are good enough. We deny our power when we believe we can't choose how to view ourselves. When we choose to see ourselves in a positive way, we take back our power and accept personal responsibility for our futures. Victims give away their power; heroes claim it. No person or experience can take away our power without our consent.

We are all in a grand classroom where we have the opportunity to learn from our experiences. Our mistakes and failures have no power to diminish us if we choose to learn from them. We can focus on shame and guilt, or we can focus on the lesson we learned and let it go. We can focus on our fears and remain full of regret, discouragement, and self-hate or we can focus on living, learning, and loving. The power no one can take from us is the power to choose our attitude. No one can give us our value or take it away. Our value remains constant. We can wisely decide to value our love, goodness, kindness, and determination, or we can unwisely place our value on our accomplishments, how we compare to others, or by the wealth we accumulate. When we're constantly learning, no experience is wasted. Time, on the other hand, is the true wealth. We waste valuable time when we focus on anything but love.

Rewriting Our Lives

I am an author. I write books. I choose the characters, and I decide how the plot plays out. I decide what material to include. Because the book is my creation, there will never be another one just like it. My story will always be unique because I am. When I'm writing, I may try out a plot or character, then later decide I don't like what those elements are doing to the story. I often go back and take out a scene or a character that isn't working. If something is not pushing the main character toward the final ending I have envisioned, I take it out. I change the plot and the characters whenever I feel it is best for the end I have in mind.

It works the same way with real life. As the author of my own life, I need to envision the end of my story as I'm living it. This vision will give me direction and purpose. I'm the one who needs to decide what is most important. I'm the one who plans out the chapters. Because I have a clear concept of the purpose of my life, I must make sure each page is getting me where I want to go. I choose the theme. I decide how to overcome the obstacles in my path. I decide how to resolve the conflicts I face. Without a clear vision, I am at the mercy of circumstances and unseemly characters that do not want me to succeed.

What many readers usually don't realize is that I rewrite every book multiple times. I always change the plot and characters in the writing process. I never get it right the first time. If I didn't rewrite my story numerous times, no one would ever publish the book, and no one would ever read it. I have to be willing to take many hard looks at my work, decide how to make it better, and rewrite it over and over again. The writing does not make the story or book worth reading; the rewriting does. The first draft is not the most important; the final draft is.

It works the same way with real living. It takes a lot of rewriting to get our personal stories right. Our early decisions and choices don't have to be our last. What happens to us is not as important as how we respond, and we can change how we respond at any time. We can step back and take an objective look at how our stories are going and see if we still respect our initial responses. If we don't like the direction our lives are going, we can make changes. We can take out a character that is harming our personal growth. We can change our response to a difficult situation because we know better now. With increased wisdom gleaned from personal experience, we can create a more peaceful and loving home. We can deliberately craft our own private tragedy or triumph.

No one writes our story for us or forces us to accept the story they want us to live without our consent. We write it and we live it. Then hopefully we rewrite our story numerous times so we don't have to relive it. In essence, we are the authors, editors, and publishers. The synopsis on the back cover will read pretty much like our obituary.

Is a life of love worth fighting for? You better believe it. The most important battles we will ever fight will always be within. Are we ready to win the war for our personal peace of mind and inner joy? Yes! No one else really knows the inner demons we face. No one understands what we have gone through or the depth of fear that holds us back. No one knows how disillusioned or disappointed we are. No one knows the terrifying doubts we feel. No one understands the deepest desires of our hearts. Only we know our personal Goliaths.

If we are willing to learn from our mistakes, no Goliath can hold us back. No great saga has a main character that remains paralyzed forever in naiveté or fear. No poignant story has a hero that stays in the clutches of those who seek to destroy. As readers, we always root for the underdog. We want the oppressed to overcome and conquer. We want good to triumph over evil. We want the oppressors to be held accountable for their actions. We want the main character to have the opportunity to love and be loved. Now is the time to cheer for ourselves. Now is the time to triumph over the negative influences in our lives. We are the only ones who can put down the pen and give up. We are the only one who can rewrite the ending of our story with persistence, hard work, courage, and faith.

There are certainly some complex and difficult situations where those involved in destructive relationships fear for their safety or the well-being of their children. If we let this fear stop us from doing the right thing, the results are even more tragic. One woman told me she felt she couldn't end her abusive marriage without putting her children at risk.

> I fell in love with a man who grew up on one of the Polynesian islands. He was everything I dreamed of. But it wasn't long after we married that he started disappearing for days at a time. Eventually I learned he was living a double life; one with me and another with his mistress. I was devastated. His father was the same way. I guess he thought that was normal. When he is home, he's abusive. I want to leave the marriage, but I'm afraid he will take the kids back to the island and I'll never see them again because his father controls who gets a visa in that country.

Community, church, and professional resources are available to any person who feels trapped in an abusive marriage. A whole army of people is standing by to help if we believe that our leaving will put us or our children at risk. But we must step forward and ask for it. We must be willing to do what it takes to keep ourselves and our children safe from the devastating effects of abuse and neglect. Every time we don't do something because we are afraid, we are making the wrong choice.

Some of us feel trapped in extended family relationships where abuse and neglect is multigenerational and keeps getting worse. Dysfunctional families constantly mired in one toxic drama after another always continue the saga to a tragic end. When family members do not love each other and in fact abuse and neglect each other, the ultimate resolution of the plot is disastrous. Sometimes we hold on to destructive relationships because of family connections even though we know they are destructive. We feel obligated to maintain close ties because our abusers are our parents, spouse, brother, or sister. Just because someone is related to us doesn't give him or her a green light to mistreat us. Abuse and neglect are wrong, and we're part of the problem if we keep putting up with them.

One woman described the moment when she finally admitted that she'd been maintaining relationships with abusive and neglectful extended family members for years, hoping that one day they would finally love her.

> The night of my daughter's wedding reception, I looked around and saw that no one from my extended family had bothered to attend—not my parents, brothers, sisters, aunts, uncles, or cousins. It wasn't just their physical absence that was a rude awakening. There were no letters or cards, phone calls, or any contact at all to congratulate my daughter. I'd spent my life trying to be a loving daughter, sister, niece, or aunt—fruitlessly trying to keep close loving connections with my family. That was the night when it dawned on me that I was doing all the work and nothing was coming back. I really didn't want to think about it, and I sure didn't want to feel as bad as I felt. But in the end, I did. I faced reality. The family members I'd sincerely loved my whole life, didn't love me. It hurt and I had to grieve the loss.
>
> I quietly stopped initiating contact. Not surprisingly, the only communication that came back after that was one sister who wrote to tell me how much she hated me, another family member who threatened legal action, and my father, who told me I was going to hell. It was hard to face the fact that I didn't mean anything to any of them, but I finally did. My family has been stuck in the effects of multigenerational abuse and neglect for generations. If I want to be mentally healthy, I can't be part of it any more. Today I'm at peace even though I can't have a close relationship with any of them. Actually, I never did. I was fooling myself. Now I'm facing reality. Now I'm free to work on creating the loving family I long for with my husband, children, and grandchildren.

Family is not always related by blood. Family is the people you love *and* are loved by. Most of the time we think our world will fall apart if we end abusive and neglectful relationships, especially with family members. But the threat and fear reside only in our thoughts. Our mind makes a family member's power over us seem very real. We imagine the worst-case scenario. We often believe those who abuse and neglect us have more control over us than they really do. At some point we have to realize that it is time to stop chasing after love, affection, and attention from those who abuse and neglect us. If love, affection, and attention are not given freely, they aren't worth having.

Those who mistreat others are troubled adults who are intent at making our lives as miserable as theirs. Sometimes when we choose to leave a relationship, those who mistreat us will threaten, make false accusations, and initiate legal proceedings. Most of the time, they simply do nothing because the power they had over us was only the power we gave them. We can't control what they do. The only people we control are us. In the long run, those who choose to maintain only healthy relationships come out on top. When we choose love over fear, peace of mind over constant drama, and self-respect over domination and control, we have the opportunity to create truly authentic and meaningful lives.

So start dreaming of the life you truly desire. Imagine what it would feel like to love and be loved. See yourself sitting around a dinner table, talking to people you love and who love you back. Imagine yourself laughing and feeling relaxed. Feel gentle loving arms around you. Envision specific people as supporting characters cheering you on instead of tearing you down. Visualize someone special in the crowd smiling up at you.

Open your mind and soul to the tender hearts of the children around you who need you to face reality and be strong. Find the strength and courage to do the right thing for them and for you. Look into the future and see the beautiful faces of your posterity desperately pleading with you to do the right thing. We cannot accept mistreatment without harming them. We have to be the force for good and stand up for all that is wholesome, kind, and innocent. We have to be defenders of love.

See your body and soul as radiant, one-of-a-kind, and glorious beyond description. Sense the warmth of emerging courage surging through your veins. Open your eyes to the beauties all around and inside you. Know in your soul that you deserve genuine affection and devotion. You are capable of offering and receiving ardent friendship and tenderness. You can create a beautiful life in which you both give and receive true love.

Creation is holy work. Visualize yourself creating a delightful life in which you spread rays of love like sunshine everywhere you go. Know that when you are free of destructive relationships, you can perform your life's work with increased energy and skill. See all the negative labels you have previously accepted about yourself falling away piece by piece until your soul is free at last. Feel your heart open to truth. Visualize your fear as the locked door that is holding you back from the light inside you. See yourself fighting your worst fear with the sword of love. No one can take the love you feel for them away from you even if you must leave them for your own safety and well-being.

See yourself walking away from all that limits your ability to love and be loved. See your personal dragon of fear diminish in size and scope to the puny and despicable powerless form of a childish nightmare. For now you are fully awake. Now you have grown to manhood and womanhood. Now you see what frightens you as a mountain you can climb or obstacle you can overcome. Now you are reborn to awareness, strength, and courage. Now you maintain only the relationships where you are treated with kindness and respect. Now you are who you really are and always have been. Now you know you are a son or daughter of God who was created to love and be loved. Anything less is not good enough anymore.

Begin your true work. Write down your dreams. Imagine your life in the future knowing that you have everything you need to be happy and content. Listen to the quiet voice inside you. Now is the time to act. Get your house in order by creating a quiet, reflective time for restoring your strength. Trust that everything will turn out all right if you are true to yourself. Count your blessings and get ready to scatter joy.

Choose to see the whole world full of people just waiting to know and appreciate you. Also choose to see the world full of people you want to know and appreciate. Many souls know how to love and be loved, and you can find them. Imagine yourself finding someone to love who is capable of loving you in return. See yourself reaching out in love and feeling love coming back to you. It is possible. But first you have to believe.

In the classic tale of the little mermaid, the main character has to give up everything she has and knows to gain a human soul. We too have to give up a former life of abuse and neglect for the opportunity to experience real human love. Someone is always trying to keep us from that treasure, but we will conquer our adversaries as long as the motivation for everything we do is love.

The ocean tides retreat and return, leaving behind treasures on the shore. If we send out love, eventually love will return. We will find buried riches hidden deep in the sun-warmed sand. Our love, buffeted by the rocks and storms of life, will return to us even more polished than the love we have given.

Now that's a story worth living.

Questions to Answer

Some of us unknowingly use our religious faith as an excuse to stay in abusive and neglectful relationships. We confuse forgiveness with tolerating abuse. Some of us believe that if we love an abuser, we must stay in the relationship. If we really love our abuser we will hold them accountable for their behavior. Losing a relationship with a parent or partner is difficult but staying in a destructive relationship is tragic.

We reward abusive and neglectful behavior when we doubt our worth. Each of us deserves to be treated with kindness and respect. If we have grown complacent or discouraged and believe our life will never get better, it is time to act. When our relationships keep us from the warmth, love, and the dignity of self-respect, it is time for change.

Consider the following questions while analyzing relationships.

- Do I maintain relationships with family members I know to be abusive and neglectful because I don't want to "cause trouble" or "break up" my family?
- Do I understand that abuse and neglect destroy families, not my decision to end a destructive relationship?
- Do I allow my children to be alone with a family member I know to be capable of abuse and neglect?
- Do I minimize the abuse and neglect in my childhood so that I can continue a relationship with a family member at all costs?

- Am I true to the quiet voice inside me that tells me someone is not good for me or my children to be around?
- Do I maintain relationships with those who control me through guilt, fear, rejection, or abandonment?
- Do I know what a healthy loving relationship looks and feels like?
- Do I often abandon myself as I try to appease those who abuse and neglect me?
- Can I trust myself to stand up for me when others abuse or neglect me?
- Do I understand that if I continue the abuse and neglect I have known, I am responsible for the damage that is done to the next generation?
- Do I take responsibility for my response to abuse and neglect?
- Do I enjoy getting sympathy from coworkers, neighbors, and friends for the abuse and neglect I am tolerating?
- Do I make excuses for why I stay in a relationship where I am abused and neglected?
- Have I written my personal story in a way that makes abuse and neglect tolerable and acceptable?
- Am I afraid to begin a new life because I don't think I can make it on my own?
- Am I considering the multigenerational model I have become?
- Will my posterity use me as a model of courage and strength or a model of inaction and cowardice?
- Do I understand that being a good husband or wife includes holding my partner accountable for their behavior?
- Do I protect my children from those who can harm them and me?

- Do I see myself as strong and decisive?
- Do I want a better life but don't know how to get there?
- Have I asked for help from my church minister, community advocate, or professional counselor?
- Do I have a plan to improve my life?
- How do I want my story to end?
- Do I care about myself and my life enough to change?
- Why do I want to continue relationships with those who use, mistreat, abuse, neglect, and reject me?
- Do I love myself?
- Do I believe that I am worthy of love?
- Have I tried to envision a life for myself that includes people to love and be loved by?
- Am I afraid to be alone?
- Have I learned how to love and be loved?

Section Five

Releasing Neglect

Chapter Nine
GIFTS FROM PAIN

If we live in destructive relationships, we experience pain that doesn't remotely feel like a gift. We hold on to our relationship for many good reasons. We hope things will get better. But things don't get better; they get worse. Now we decide what road to take. It's never too late to turn the page and begin a new chapter. When something bad happens to us, we are always free to choose how we respond. As a result of our choice, a destructive relationship can define, destroy, or strengthen us.

What happened yesterday has no power over us. In fact, yesterday is a merely a compilation of early plot development scenes leading to this moment. The gifts from pain start arriving when we actually learn from our experiences. When we know better, we can make wiser choices. If we hold on to our victimhood, we will eventually destroy everything we treasure in life. The heartbreak we experience is wasted if we don't accept the gifts that pain has to offer.

THE MOMENT OF DECISION

This is the moment when our choices can't stay the same. This is when we decide if all we desire is won or lost. We face the reality of our life with truth and courage, or we submit to domination and despair. Everything will be different after we make a decision and take action. Today is the day to face our personal dragons no matter the cost. Our children and our children's children are cheering for us, hoping beyond hope that we will not give in or give up.

We don't have to feel foolish because of our failure to act before now. We are stronger because of what we have experienced. We survived in the past with creative and powerful defenses such as denial, dissociation, repression, or fantasy. These defenses kept us alive and sane when we were too young, weak, or uninformed to make better choices. Now we can find the necessary support and resources to heal and move forward. We are not doomed to fall into a private hell of mental illness, suicide, or self-destructive choices. We do not have to leave a tragic legacy of victimhood for those who follow.

Each event in our lives tutors us if we are eager and humble students. In the past, we have not protected ourselves; now is the time to stop this self-betrayal. As we leave our victimhood behind, we are also free to let go of resentment, anger, self-pity, and offended feelings. If we stay in the healing process long enough, we will rediscover and liberate parts of ourselves that were lost. We will reclaim our innocence. We will relearn how to relax, play, laugh, trust, create, and love. These are the attributes of the innocent child we once were. These can be the attributes of the mature adult we are becoming.

All great stories are fraught with danger and characters that cannot be trusted. But the stories that move us always involve overcoming tragedy and evil at great odds. If we're not learning anything from our experiences, we're trapped in a plot that leads to tragedy. Nothing is more frustrating for a reader than a main character in a story who does nothing. It is difficult to keep rooting for a good guy who doesn't even try to get out of harm's way. When we truly care about a character, we long for him to face his foe with courage, no matter the cost.

If we metaphorically step out of our own life story for a moment, we have the opportunity to develop the perspective we need to see our circumstances with greater clarity. We increase our chances of seeing things the way they really are. Additional possibilities for course corrections and happier chapters will come to mind. We develop the ability to more quickly identify friend or foe and face our adversaries with boldness. We see better life choices for ourselves. Then we can answer the following questions with positive affirmations and hope:

- "Do I like me?"
- "Do I like the direction my life is headed?"
- "What would I like to see me do differently?"
- "What will I say to myself at my darkest moment of despair?"
- "How do I want my story to end?"
- "What do I need to do differently to get to my happy ever after?"

If we are not satisfied with the quality of our relationships, it is time to imagine a brand-new narrative. Before a main character can make wise choices, he needs access to his own inner wisdom. This personal insight summons inner daring and tells us who is friend and foe. If we have not learned from our past, we are doomed to relive it. Only when we embrace our own inner wisdom and respond differently to the people and circumstances in our lives are we free to begin living the next chapter. Then we can find the simple joy in living that is ready and waiting for everyone.

Because of what we've gleaned from our past experiences, we can choose to respond differently now. We have changed. We are not the same person we once were. At the same time, we give ourselves permission to be a work in progress. We patiently allow ourselves to learn from our mistakes and the mistreatment of others. It is the direction we are heading, not where we've been, that is important.

We'll never leave where we are until we can dream or imagine where we'd rather be. All real change begins in our minds and in our hearts; a change in behavior follows. We can move into a new chapter of our lives by focusing our energy on the only people we can control . . . us. We access our inner power when we move from thinking and dreaming and take decisive action. We need to trust that good things are ahead for us no matter how dark our life seems today. When we make difficult choices in the present, we ease the burdens of those who follow us. The strongest souls, the most compassionate characters, emerge as the result of pain. There is no way around, only through. We become stronger and more compassionate when we feel our sorrow, allow that heartache to change us for the good, and then choose to move forward and live meaningful lives in which we love and are loved.

Becoming a Chain-Breaker

We can become the chain breakers that stop abuse and neglect in our families. We can absorb the poison but refuse to pass it on. We neutralize the poison we were given when we decide that our children will not receive the familial pain that was given to us. We can choose to give love even though we have not received love. We can choose to experience joy though we have known great sorrow. Unless we face facts and see things the way they really are, the ongoing abuse and neglect will ripple outward from one generation to the next unchecked. Someone has to comprehend the continuing tragedy and say, "This is real! This is wrong. *I* must stop it! Abuse and neglect end with me."

One woman described the day when she decided she had to confront a difficult reality and end a relationship with her father.

> When I was in my forties, an estranged sister reunited with the family long enough to tell us she had been sexually abused by my father while she was growing up. My father denied the accusations. I didn't know who to believe. Still I took precautions. I did not allow my children to be around my dad after that accusation unless I was in the same room with them. I felt all right about my decision because it seemed impossible to choose between my sister and my father. I wanted both of them in my life.
>
> Several months later, my father came over to my house without my stepmother when he knew I was home alone. My husband was at work and all my children were in school. He tried to get me to look at his private parts. Even though he gave me some medical excuse, his request made me feel disgusted. When I refused, he accused me of being a failure as a daughter. Then he came by several weeks later when I was home alone and tried the same thing. That is when I knew I couldn't possibly maintain a relationship with him any longer without putting myself and my children at risk.
>
> My previous relationship with my father was full of many long years of continual neglect. He only made contact with me when he needed something. I kept trying to get his attention and affection, but he seemed fixated on certain sisters. When I suddenly realized why, I felt so sick to my stomach that I threw up. I had been holding on to the hope of receiving my father's love for my entire life. I felt responsible to fix the problems in my family. I wanted my children to have a loving relationship with their grandparents because I never had. Now I knew that would never be possible. I was not safe and my children were not safe. If I continued a relationship, I put future generations at risk. So I stopped initiating contact. My father only tried to connect with me once after that. He sent me a letter disclaiming responsibility for my sister's accusations, stating that I had no right to divorce him and made a veiled threat to my physical and spiritual safety.

Many people feel guilty that they didn't recognize abuse and neglect and do something about it sooner. We feel foolish for hanging on to a desperate need to be loved. When we are survivors of abuse and neglect, adding guilt to our long list of negative feelings about ourselves does little good. It is time to applaud ourselves for finally figuring out the sordid mess and taking steps to protect ourselves and our children. Too many of us remain in a multigenerational pattern of avoidance and inaction, thinking we are "honoring" our parents or our marriage vows. We continue to sweep abuse and neglect under the rug. Until someone pulls back the rug and faces the dirt under there, nothing gets better and it can get a whole lot worse.

Because we always choose our response to being neglected and abused, it helps to look closely at our present behavior. We can learn to view our interactions through a clear lens. Sometimes we try to keep the peace at the price of personal honesty and self-respect. Dealing with the truth, no matter how dark, it always better in the long run.

One woman described her struggles with abuse and neglect throughout her life along with the resulting personal regret this way:

> I'm a people pleaser. I stayed married to a man who is a philanderer and an alcoholic because I didn't want to be alone. I couldn't see how I could support us by myself even though he never adequately provided for us anyway. We lived off welfare and handouts. Now I see that my refusal to leave my marriage hurt me, my children, *and* my husband. My children paid the price for my failure to protect them from their father. My husband had no reason to change because he was never held accountable. I live with the regret that I could have made a better life for all of us. We were like a bunch of frogs thrown in a pan of warm water. The temperature kept getting hotter and hotter, but I wasn't smart enough to get us all out of there before we all got burned. Now all my children are involved in abusive relationships or in jail. I have to take part of the responsibility

for that. I live alone now and support myself. It is not as hard as I thought it would be. I wish I'd left sooner. I was neglected as a child, and I think I was just used to being treated that way. I was so focused on my pain that I didn't see the damage being done to my children. My choice haunts me.

WHAT WE LEARN FROM DEPRESSION

Depression is common in those who have been mistreated. Some depression is the result of unfelt and unhealed childhood abuse and neglect, so understanding our past may be a puzzle solver for our present mental health issues. It helps to know that there is a difference between depressed thinking, which we can learn to avoid, and depressed feelings, which sometimes must be felt. Depressed feelings are a signal that something is wrong, and we need to pay attention and figure out what it is.

Depression can be thought of as an invitation to give up something or someone in our life that is not good for us. If we have been neglected or abused, depression can be a message from our own soul pleading for change. Something deep inside us wants to heal the abandonment or rejection we experienced. Depression is sometimes a signal from the child we once were who longs for us to take action now as adults. We need to give ourselves permission to feel. If we can feel, we can heal. We usually dismiss what we are feeling or add guilt to the heap of unfelt emotions.

There are two kinds of depression—necessary suffering, which can be thought of as healthy depression, and unnecessary suffering, which includes inner hopelessness, shame, regret, and fear. If we stay physically present to the sensations of sadness and fear we feel in the present, they will lessen in time. We can relive our abandonment experience and work through it instead of launching into full-blown panic attacks. We can learn to put the abuse or neglect we experienced into proper perspective and learn something from what we experienced. We can learn to comfort the abandoned or terrified child who was once us.

Abuse and neglect can be the most devastating of all life experiences, but healing is possible. Healing happens when we allow ourselves to experience all our emotions and then learn to manage them. We can't ignore our feelings without damaging our mental health. If we have experienced a loss of trust, innocence, and personal boundaries, this pain must be acknowledged and mourned. Mourning is required to relieve pain. Then we can move forward and replace self-pity with nurturing attention.

The following are healthy ways to nurture ourselves.

- Write about our experiences and feelings in a journal or letter.
- See ourselves as nurturing adults.
- Express anger in a safe place (work out at the gym).
- Break the silence (tell your story to someone who will listen with compassion).
- Attend counseling sessions or join a support group
- Strive to understand where our feelings are coming from.
- Understand why we may have difficulties with trust or intimacy.
- See if you are addicted to something as a way to deal with the unfelt pain.
- Remember that forgiveness is not forgetting but remembering in peace.

Why Is Pain Necessary?

One way pain helps us is that it forces us to wake up and pay attention. We go to the doctor when we are in physical pain. When we are in emotional pain, we can go to our inner physician. That light inside each of us begs us to find, face, and feel the truth about our lives. Emotional pain won't just disappear. No antibiotic will rid us of this kind of infection. Our emotional immune system, not unlike our physical immune system, must mobilize with inner courage and honesty. There must be a figurative lancing of the infection site. In other words we are going to hurt a lot for a while before we are going to feel better. Feeling repressed grief helps us work through denial, awareness, justice, empowerment, and ultimately moves us toward forgiveness and healing.

Our souls each figuratively have four rooms we need to access every day if we want to discover our authentic selves, or our souls made visible. In one room, the physical part of our souls reside, needing us to eat healthy food and get adequate rest and exercise. In another room is the mental part of our souls that need us to continue learning, growing, and challenging ourselves. The emotional part of our souls is in another room and need us to laugh, rest, and develop close associations with loving family members and friends. Finally the spiritual part of our souls needs quiet moments of meditation and a sacred place to recover from the stress of life. When we neglect to access these rooms every day because we are avoiding pain, we stop growing and improving. We merely exist. We live in quiet desperation and hide constant feelings of inadequacy and hopelessness. If we face reality and visit each room each day, we free ourselves to continue down the road of growth and maturity.

GIFTS OF PAIN

Pain does not prevent a meaningful life; in fact, pain enhances our joy. We can't have one without the other. We don't often think of pain as a gift, yet pain can be a life-changing opportunity. Pain gives us:

Understanding

When we are not loved by those we love, we quickly learn the damage to our soul caused by abuse and neglect because we have experienced it. If we actually feel our pain, we will be less likely to treat someone without respect and kindness because we know how it feels.

Empathy

We understand how much our partners and children need love when we have experienced the pain of not having our love returned. We see their needs as our own because we can put ourselves in their shoes. We do not want others to be in pain so we behave in ways that will demonstrate our love and ease their burdens.

Love

All the love we feel is never wasted even when it is not returned. The pain of unrequited love comes back to us and creates a ready reservoir in our own souls. The ability to love and be loved is the quest and reward of a lifetime of practice. There are always deeper and more meaningful ways to love. A deep respect for our own soul and for the souls of others moves us to action. For real love is what we do not just how we feel. When we love someone, we serve him in the ways he needs to be served.

Knowledge of Good and Evil

When those who might have loved us choose to abuse and neglect us, we've known darkness and evil. Experiencing this kind of deep personal pain allows us to more fully appreciate peace, joy, and love. Then when we know both good and evil and choose good, of our own free will, a light in the darkness of this world is lit inside us and never goes out.

Compassion

If we have experienced rejection, abandonment, abuse, and neglect, we look for hidden anguish in others with greater sensitivity. It is difficult to understand what others have gone through unless we have experienced it ourselves. Compassion born of personal experience allows us to feel what others feel.

Benevolence

When those closest to us knowingly withhold love from us, we have felt great sorrow. We can choose to respond to this sorrow by becoming people who give others love. We can choose benevolence and generosity as our personal response to abuse and neglect.

Kindheartedness

When those we love don't love us, we can decide to become the loving people we've always longed for ourselves and for someone else. We can choose to become more sensitive and caring. A light and softness comes to the countenance of those who choose to live in love. Kindness, gentleness, and sympathy are gifts we offer others after a deep thoughtful choice to give to others what was denied to us.

AVOIDING PAIN

Most people involved in destructive relationships will not leave until the pain of staying in the current relationship exceeds the pain associated with making a change. Pain is a wake-up call. Contrary to what most of us believe, the ability to feel pain actually enhances all of our varied and multifaceted experiences. If we can't feel pain, we can't feel much of anything. The inability to feel pain is a serious matter; for if we choose to avoid pain, we are creating our own private hell. For hell is not so much a place as it is a mental state of mind—an emptiness, a dark inner void where we harbor desires to control, ignore, dismiss, harm, or destroy others. If we don't feel pain, we don't have to experience regret or anguish, but neither will we feel peace and joy. If we don't feel pain, we don't have to feel sorrow or longing, but neither will we feel compassion or kindness.

The desire to avoid pain is the source of much mental illness and man's inhumanity to man. Only through pain do we learn compassion and understand how others feel. Only through pain do we access the creative and healing energy of the universe. Without the ability to feel pain, we live in dark shadows, empty and soulless. We live with a constant craving to compare, compete, and control those around us. We initiate unnecessary conflict and obsess about ways to harm or destroy those we might have loved.

The baptism of pain allows us to enter into the holy sacrament of the present moment. We are no longer blind and dumb. We clearly see our own true motives in stark reality along with the genuine motives of others. Pain frees us. We are not bound in regrets from the past or anxiety about the future. We are fully present in the glorious now. We look for and find abundance instead of scarcity everywhere we look. Our lives become genuine prayers of gratitude. We create genuine wealth by forming loving family ties. We create beauty from ashes by changing the course of our own lives. We create meaningful and fulfilling lives as we become the blessings in the lives of others that we seek for ourselves.

CREATING A BETTER LIFE

Creating a beautiful life is holy work, but it *is* work. The silk pillow and endless chocolate bon-bon idea of heaven is not real. Happiness is really a state of mind along with the ability to honor both our own needs and the needs of those around us. There is no security in material possessions or worldly honors. Serenity comes from creating a meaningful life of service, the ability to trust those closest to you, and the giving and receiving of compassion and kindness. Because life is always movement and change, the pain we feel today is inevitable but fleeting. Pain diminishes over time if we make choices that lead to genuine love. When we choose to feel it all—gain and loss—our pain will be our loving teacher and friend.

Though we seldom like to think about it, we are all going to die. We don't know when our time is up. Each day could be our last. So it follows that we must not waste time. Before our story ends, we can choose to fill our life with love. If the way we are living and the relationships we are involved in are not bringing us peace and joy, we can choose something better. Choosing to love someone who is capable of loving us in return is one way to create a bit of heaven right now.

We always have the power to give love; we do not, however, have the power to make others love us back. Yet even when our love is not returned, the love we feel inside will transform us, become us. There is a simple but true universal story—in the end, we always receive what we give and reap what we sow.

We have been the ugly duckling, and now we are the beautiful swan. Those who don't see our beauty no longer have any power over us. We have become who we were born to be. Pain is a hard teacher, but if we learn from pain, it is our dearest friend. We are the authors who choose to craft our private tragedies or masterpieces. The simple love story or sordid tale of our lives is our own creation.

Chapter Ten

DISCOVERING JOY

Creating meaningful lives is our highest mission. We can't fulfill our mission unless we deal with the relationships we are involved in today. Changing our response to destructive relationships is hard, but once we take that leap of courage, change is liberating. No bird learns to fly in an outgrown nest. None of us grows in our ability to love and be loved as long as we remain in relationships where we cannot practice the art of love. If we are not experiencing joy, we can change our story by changing us.

Many of us live much like Rapunzel, locked in a tower, waiting for some unknown hero to save us. In real life, we have to save ourselves. We can take that first courageous leap into the unknown by simply believing a better life is possible. Then we take positive action. We literally walk away from anything that seeks to destroys our dignity and self-respect or hinders the full expression of our potential. We can leave the dark night and wake up to the light of a new day and a brighter future. When we are motivated by love—not fear or revenge—we become bold and beautiful.

THE WORTH OF OUR OWN SOULS

When we fully understand the worth of a soul, including our own, we see all humanity with an increased measure of awe. The worth of each soul is immeasurable. When we take the heart of another person in our hands, we stand on holy ground. How we choose to treat ourselves and those around us is the final essence of our lives. At the end, what matters is not what we got but what we gave, not how well known we were but whether we had a positive influence in the lives of those closest to us. Our value is not in possessions, power, or prestige, but in our goodness, humanity, service, and charity. If we want to live in a way that matters, we will live motivated by love.

No matter what has happened in our past, we decide what we want from our lives today. One clear truth we all discover is that joy and pain are connected. We can't have one without the other. If we can't feel pain, we can't feel joy. We will experience the fulness of joy we're meant to have when *we* become the person we've always longed to have in our life, give to others what was denied to us, and respect ourselves enough to walk away from destructive relationships. We always have a choice.

"I just wanted someone to love me."

As I've interviewed hundreds of people during my writing career, this desperate desire was what motivated many to make soul-damaging choices concerning their relationships. Why does this universal longing to be loved so often lead us to make unwise choices in our closest relationships? A desire to be loved is not bad. But if our desire to be loved is desperate, we won't take the time to understand what love is before we choose to give our hearts to those who cannot love us in return. We won't take the time to know and accept ourselves, to nurture and fill our own needs. We won't take the time to become loving people first so that we can discern the true motives in others.

We won't be truly loved until we become truly loving people.

Too often we search for love out there when what we really need is love in here. Before we can access our inner reservoirs, we need reflective time to think and ponder what it means to love. We need time to see and understand that love is service and sacrifice; we serve and sacrifice for those we love. As we evaluate and quietly listen to our hearts, we will make better choices concerning those who are capable of love. We will stop waiting for love and start becoming people who know how to give and receive love.

It is difficult to become loving people when we are embroiled in damaging associations. When we walk away from destructive relationships, we discover a new world that has always existed, but we couldn't see it because we were asleep. We've been living in black and white, but now everything takes on added brightness and color. When we live a life of love, our senses rediscover the brilliance we once knew as children. We find ourselves relishing the small things like the sound of a stranger's laughter, the smell of fresh baked bread, or the gentle touch of a child's hand. We are able to see and feel our lives for the miracle they really are. Little by little, we wake from soul-numbing slumber. A life-changing sense of gratitude begins to soak into every cell of our bodies.

LEARNING HOW TO LOVE

We will eventually experience grace if our greatest quest is learning how to love and be loved. We will connect with a power beyond ourselves that enlarges our capacities. As we practice loving ourselves and others, we will have difficult days. We will find that our love is not always returned. Yet as we continue to learn and grow, we become wiser and softer. We understand that we can always keep those we love in our hearts, but we can't always keep them in our lives. Even though we can't keep them in our lives, the love we have felt for them is never diminished even when it is not reciprocated. All love eventually flows back to the person who loves and fills the soul with peace. All the love we've ever felt is alive inside us, expanding our ability to feel compassion, tenderness, charity, and devotion with even greater depth as the years go by. Even when our love is not returned, pain gives us understanding and empathy. Then we know:

- I am enough. You are enough.
- I am not alone. You are not alone.
- I am loved. You are loved.

Undoubtedly we will be discouraged during the hard part of our story. We will feel deep sorrow when those we love don't love us. If we don't give up and keep choosing to love, we will eventually create beautiful and meaningful lives. Nothing really changes in our stories until *we* change. Our relationships and circumstances may change, but unless *we* change, we keep living in a circle, repeating what we have done in the past and going nowhere. Personal change is not easy or painless.

First, we'll need to overcome all that discourages us. The things others do and say only have the power we give them to hurt us. A sense of gratitude for all we have and all we are comes only when we listen to that quiet inner voice inside that tells us we are worthy of love. We have an endless reservoir of tenderness inside us to share. We don't have to be afraid of being alone. Peace of mind comes at a price. That price is personal courage and self-respect.

While pain is inevitable of all of us, how we respond is optional. We can choose continued suffering or healing forgiveness. We can choose self-determination and independence or domination and submission. Any relationship that crushes the self-respect and inner light and joy of another human being must be carefully examined and eliminated. Decisions must be made. The time of fear is over. The time of courage has begun.

So much of inhumanity in this world is the misuse of power. When we refuse to misuse the power we have over others, we have the capacity to literally change the world for good. Love won't fail us if we never stop loving. Yet to love is to risk rejection. To love is to risk abandonment. To love is to risk loss. Even then, love is still worth it, for real love is never lost. Even when it is not returned, love flows back into the one who loves and heals the broken heart.

Love also includes the pain of personal transformation by the opening of our eyes. If we choose to love, we won't be naked and naïve in the Garden of Eden any longer. For we have chosen to partake of the forbidden fruit. We can't choose to love without also knowing pain and being profoundly changed. If we embrace personal change instead of running from it, we will be given a glimpse of heaven right here and now. The essence of a meaningful life involves the triumph of light over darkness.

At the end of our lives, will we be able to say:

- "I have lived an authentic life."
- "I have learned."
- "I have loved."
- "By the grace of God, I have created a beautiful and meaningful life."

Personal Change

See Ourselves Accurately

Before we can feel joy, we need to know how wonderful we already are. Most of us who have been abused and neglected have a hard time loving ourselves. No matter how much good we do or how much we accomplish, we feel inadequate and defective. We need to feel our own value in the core of our souls. We need to know that our worth is infinite and absolute. We need to know that nothing we do or don't do changes our value. We need to know that nothing someone says or does can diminish us. We have irreplaceable and infinite souls. Feeling our great worth is a personal choice. No one else can give us this intrinsic sense of value, we must choose to see our worth and feel our value. By our own free will and choice, we must choose to recognize our indomitable significance.

See Others Accurately

It is common for those who have been abused and neglected to make excuses for the people who mistreat them. We need to see others in reality and insist that they are accountable for their behavior. When we remove ourselves from destructive relationships, we don't have to play the role of judge and jury. We simply move forward with our lives because we have learned that trust is earned, and this person cannot be trusted. Even a small child on a playground has the good sense after being mistreated to say, "I don't want to play with you 'cause you're mean to me." We can empathize with those who choose to abuse and neglect others, but we must never condone or excuse their negative behavior. Their choices are providing them with opportunities to learn. When we make self-destructive choices, we need to take responsibility for them if we are going to learn from them.

After we've left an abusive relationship, we will continue to have emotional problems if we continue to rehash the wrongs against us. Those who abuse and neglect others are also suffering. We can hope they will change their behavior and have a better life in the future even if that life will not include us. The emotional scars from the past will never heal if they become our thoughts and accusations in the present. Part of forgiveness is the giving up the right to hold a grudge. When we react to adversity in a self-absorbed way, we become like our adversity. We want bad things to happen to those who have abused us. We have no right to wish harm on others even if they have gravely harmed us. Hell is a state of mind, or the craving to injure others.

See Abusive Relationships Accurately

It is difficult to grow up and accept responsibility for our relationships. The truth is, it takes two to form a relationship, and we're always half of the equation. It follows that our acceptance of abusive and neglectful behavior is half the problem. We have to accept responsibility for our half of destructive relationships and learn something from our mistakes. Every person in our lives provides us with a lesson. Every association is a teacher. When we look at our relationships this way, we will be less likely to be drawn into drama we didn't create and can't fix. As we look forward to new or improved relationships, it is important to answers questions such as:

- "How do I create relationships where the first priority is mutual love and concern?"
- "How do I overcome my fear and submission?"
- "Is it possible to forgive but still choose to leave a relationship?"
- "Does forgiving means I need to maintain a relationship with this person?"
- "How long does it take to forgive?"
- "Can this pain eventually be transformed into love?

Often we have a hard time appraising our relationship honestly and objectively. It helps to talk to friends and counselors who will guide us and help us decide if we are seeing matters realistically. Understanding our relationships through the objectivity of someone who is not emotionally attached can be a real eye-opener. One man told me about the effects of an abusive relationship in his childhood:

> I was abused by a family friend when I was a young. I didn't tell my parents. I spun out of control when I was a teenager; did everything to put my own life at risk. I didn't really care if I died because maybe that would take the pain away. I didn't care who I hurt. I blamed myself for what happened because I did nothing to stop it. After years of basically trying to kill myself in every conceivable way, I just hit rock bottom. I finally opened up to a therapist. The biggest thing that helped me was when he said, "Look buddy, it's not your fault. You didn't cause the abuse you experienced. Something bad happened to you. But I'll tell you what is your fault . . . the way you're behaving right now and all the people you are hurting. You have to quit using that awful experience as a crutch to keep hurting yourself and everybody around you."

After Leaving

Many who have been abused and neglected get stuck even after leaving the relationship. It takes time, patience, and practice to learn the new skills of loving ourselves and others. I have enjoyed watching my ten children take piano lessons. As their parent, I never get mad at them for making a mistake and hitting the wrong key when they are practicing. I know that if they keep practicing, they will eventually get better and better. Their skill at playing the piano will improve *if they just don't stop practicing.* It works the same way in life. We don't have to get frustrated and mad at ourselves when we make mistakes. If we just keep practicing we'll learn the art of love.

The following ideas may be helpful for those of us who are striving to find a more joyful way to life.

All We Need to Be Happy

Most of us spend a lifetime looking for happiness in wealth, prestige, honors, or degrees. Happiness is the result of loving relationships. Our greatest influence will always be in our own family, even if we must live alone for a season. If our biological family is abusive, we can choose to create a loving family with our spouse and children or those individuals who we associate with in our church, work, or community. Family isn't always blood. Happiness really is a quality of thought or a state of mind. When we are at peace with ourselves and our choices, we don't depend on others to make us happy. The best way to stay happy is to let go of what makes us sad.

Listen to Our Hearts

Listening to our hearts includes recognition that a sense of abundance is our spiritual birthright. We all have so much to be grateful for. We don't have to hoard our possessions, time, or talents. The more we share, the more we have and the more we are. The more we are grateful for the everyday miracles, the more we will be given. A wasted life is a search for wealth and security. A full, rich life is a discovery of love and serenity. As we daily discover the why of everything we do, we learn to live authentic lives. The very thing we most wanted and didn't receive is the very thing we are best suited to offer to others.

Carve Out Quiet Reflective Time

Life goes by so quickly. Slow down. Relish the small things. We need solitude and time to ponder what is precious. Sit down next to yourself and listen. Meditate. Take long walks or soak in the tub. Too much of modern life is busy, chasing, fast paced, and career oriented. Talk to older people and find out what matters most before you die. What matters most should never suffer from what matters least. Keeping a record of our life in a journal is a great way to sort out the clutter and help us reorder our priorities.

Remember That Everything Will Work Out

We can relax and enjoy life more if we understand that no matter what happens, everything will eventually work out. Though our lives may seem too much to handle today, tomorrow always comes, and a new day always follows even the darkest night. It also helps to develop a relationship with a higher power and remember that we are not alone. Though life is continual challenge and change, we can trust that we learn most when confronted with the hard times.

Scatter Joy

We don't have to wait and wait for others to cheer us up. When we become the source of light in others' lives, we will immediately feel the light brighten in our own. People are so hungry for a kind word, a simple smile, a warm handshake, or a pat on the shoulder. The magical wonder of spreading joy is that it always comes back to the person who shares it.

Simplify

We can all learn to simply. One way to simplify is to figure out what we can do without. We can learn to relax and focus on *who* we want to be today not what we want to do. We can always choose joy for we have power over our inner state of mind. We don't have to do everything or be everything to keep everyone happy. Simply being us is enough. A simple life is an abundant life. There is too much of hurry and worry. We can set our own pace and march to the beat of our own drummer.

Create

We can access the creative energy of the universe by bringing forth something that wasn't there before. Each of us has a gift to share. The world needs our gifts just as much as we need to share them. In the giving and receiving, the circle of love is complete. The desire to create is one of best parts of being human. If we study every culture that has existed since the beginning of time, we will find that even in the most primitive conditions, the human heart seeks to create beauty for beauty's sake.

Discover What Brings Peace and Joy

We can learn to trust ourselves and our own instincts. When we finally own our unique point of view, we should realize how precious it is. We can study ourselves and find what brings us peace and joy. We can find a quiet time each day for contemplation, prayer, reading, hobbies, and self-regeneration. We can listen to inspiring music, volunteer at the local school or hospital, or learn a new skill. If it doesn't give us peace and joy, we can let it go.

Be Kind

The time is now to stop worrying. Guilt and stress don't get us where we want to go. We can more fully embrace our lives and each location on our individual journeys. We can be grateful for both the good and the bad experiences because we learn lessons from both. We can forgive our mistakes, be kind, and give ourselves the permission to be a work in progress. If we are alive, then we are making mistakes, for that is how we continue to learn and grow.

We can listen more acutely to the impressions that come to our hearts and minds. We can focus our energy on what we can control. We can trust that everything happens for a reason and we will make sense of everything someday. Though we can't stop bad things from happening, we can also trust that good things are on the way.

Be Strong

Difficult people teach us who we don't want to be. Become big enough to forgive but not stupid or naive enough to trust an abuser. Accept that nothing we can do can change the past. What is important is the direction we are headed. We can decide that our beginning will not be our end.

Choose Love

Love is a power greater than any other. Love is the very essence of the person who loves, not of the one who is loved. Nothing will change fundamentally until we change. We will never find a beloved until we become a lover. Even though we can't always have a relationship with those we love because of their poor choices, we can keep the love we have for them alive in us. That love will save us.

Forgive

Love discovers truths about individuals that others cannot see. When we forgive, it changes our hearts, or the way we feel about the people who harmed us. When we forgive, we are able to leave cruel relationships behind us without resentment and recrimination. Then we can love life and be free of self-pity. We won't be liberated from the burden of negative feelings for the people who hurt us unless we forgive.

Forgiving doesn't mean condoning or excusing; it means we choose to let God be the final judge. Forgiveness doesn't mean we forget; it means remembering with peace. Forgiveness is not excusing; it is letting go of accusing. When we keep accusing after we have left the relationship, we are ingesting a fatal poison. A change of circumstance will not make a difference. When we refuse to forgive we don't leave bitter feelings behind, we take them with us. Forgoing the taking of offense is the crowning achievement of the one who forgives.

Other people do not have more power over our happiness than we do. Sometimes we want to believe that other people have the ability to cause bad feelings in us and we can't do anything about it. But this pattern of thinking is false. Self-betrayal occurs when we don't do what we believe to be the right thing to do. We hold on to victimhood longer than necessary. We are free to let go of our victim status at any moment and get on with the business of living. That is how we find our happy ever after.

Forgiveness is also about choosing love over fear. We can practice the art of love by loving before we are loved in return. Our abusive relationships lose the power to harm us when we forgive. Though we can't keep abusive people in our lives, we can keep them in our hearts. We can hope that they will make better choices in the future. When we bless a situation by loving those who harm us, the cruelty of others has no more power to hurt us. When we choose compassion, fear disappears, for it is impossible to feel fear and love at the same time.

One woman spoke to me about her decision to remove herself from damaging relationships with her parents and siblings.

> The most difficult day of my life was the day I realized I couldn't stay in close relationships with my parents and brothers and sisters without risking my own life. I had been threatened with public humiliation, bodily harm, lawsuits, and even murder. Knowing that the people I loved wanted to destroy me was traumatic and soul wrenching. It almost drove me to insanity. Yet even then I could not force myself to stop loving them just because they didn't love me. So I got on my knees and

> figuratively gave them to God's keeping. I forgive them. Every day I pray for them. I love my family, perhaps even more than they love themselves. I want the best for them. I hope that their destructive and demoralizing choices will change someday, but I no longer put myself and my family at risk waiting for that to happen.

When we live in reality, we take responsibility for our own thoughts, feelings, and actions. This means that we examine our life situation honestly and refuse to shift blame for our well-being to anyone but ourselves. We are responsible to place ourselves only in relationships where there is mutual respect, love, and concern. When we choose to remove people from our lives, it doesn't mean that we hate them; it means that we respect ourselves. The common everyday actions we practice in our homes have great significance. The human soul is sacred and must be guarded and protected from all forms of abuse and neglect. We don't have to live in fear anymore. We can choose a better way to live that will allow us to rediscover our happy heart, confidence, and self-respect.

Writing the End to Our Story

Life doesn't just happen to us; we choose the end of our story. If we don't like how our story is going, we can change it by changing the main character. If we don't like the road we're on, we can choose a different path. If our focus is love, we're on a journey that eventually leads to inner peace and joy. It is important that we understand the difference between the road we're on and our destination. It may be dark and stormy on our path right now, but that doesn't mean that we aren't headed for sunshine. We need to become loving souls before we eventually attract another loving soul.

Our relationships form our character because we choose our response to every experience. Our experiences with others make us bitter or better by our own choice. It is time to stop chasing after or hating those who abandon, neglect, and abuse us. When people abuse us or walk away, let them go. The end of our story is not tied to anyone who chooses to harm us. Pronouncing final judgment on those who mistreat us is not necessary. All we need to know is that their part in our story is over and there are better relationships ahead. Those who have the capacity to love and be loved will come willingly into our lives—and stay. There is no forcing of wills in love, only freedom and serenity.

At the end of our lives, what matters most is the significant role we played in the lives of others, especially those closest to us. Have our relationships encouraged and built up others or discouraged and destroyed? Are others able to make better choices because they have interacted with us? How have we treated those in our circle of influence? What have we done with the tender hearts and the trusting souls that have been offered to us? Real success or failure does not play out in the marketplace, office, classroom, or on the playing field. Real success or failure plays out in the quiet corners of our own homes. For if we really want to live a life that matters, we will choose a life of love. The difficult people and circumstances we encounter along the way will not define or destroy us if we allow all our experiences to teach us a more principled way to live. If we live a life motivated by love, we will eventually find joy and lasting peace.

Every experience in life has a purpose; we learn that purpose if we allow ourselves to be transformed into a better person. If we are patient, focused, and positive, we will make small gradual self-improvements. Discouragement and self-doubt are part of the journey and always loom largest just before a personal breakthrough. So we must do the thing we think we can't do and embrace the pain we think we cannot bear. We must never give up on ourselves even when the odds are against us. Then we will see the blazing candle even in the bleakest night. For love is the most powerful force for light and goodness in this world. Through great love, all miracles of personal transformation are wrought.

The most important battles we will ever fight will be in our own hearts and minds. Because we are the only one who is privy to our true thoughts and deepest desires, the quality of our feelings, opinions, views, and beliefs will become the summation of our lives. When our thoughts and desires are pure—when we seek to love, bless, and create instead of control, harm and destroy—we build meaningful lives of devotion and purpose. When our benevolent outward actions mirror our inward compassionate thoughts, we will treat all men and women with kindness and respect, including ourselves. Each heart that chooses courage, personal responsibility, and love over all else has won the private battle we all must fight.

Not everyone is motived by love. We must not allow ourselves to be controlled by those motivated by anything else. Their dark desires have nothing to offer us. They are racing headlong into self-ruin; the craving to abuse and neglect others is a living hell. We have to take a stand and fight for what is right and good. When Aragorn, in J. R. R. Tolkien's *Lord of the Rings,* leads the armies of Gondor and Rohan in a march on the Black Gate of Mordor, he is outmanned and outnumbered. Still he chooses to stand and face his foe with seemingly insurmountable odds. Powers we do not now comprehend will also come to our aid in our darkest hour. There is always hope no matter what the personal cost.

Aragorn is later hailed as the conquering hero and crowned with his bride as king and queen of their kingdom. We too have a mission of importance to complete before we can be crowned kings and queens. But first, we must stay the course and engage in the daily battle that requires everything we possess—all our heart, might, mind, and strength. Though we will be wounded as we face the misuse of power multiple times in our lives, we can be sure that the supremacy of love will eventually conquer. Though our personal daily battles often seem lost, the larger war is already won. Good will triumph and love will reign. We can finish the final draft of our life story knowing full well that we gave the battle for love everything we had. We held nothing back.

Love is the essence of a meaningful life. Love isn't a fairy tale where all the loose ends are tied up with a satin ribbon at the end of the story. Love is the quiet voice at the end of the day that whispers, "Each soul has infinite value." When we truly learn to love and be loved, it is cause for great celebration. For a life filled with love is the only real happily ever after.

Questions to Answer

We must ask ourselves profound relational questions if we want to live rich and meaningful lives. Though we all have difficult circumstances and people to deal with, how we respond is always a choice. If we choose to love and be loved instead of tolerating mistreatment, we have the opportunity to experience an abundant life. How we behave toward other people really matters. How others behave toward us really matters. When we touch the soul of another human being, we walk on sacred ground.

When we choose to treat others with respect and kindness, and when we expect to be treated with respect and kindness, we each write a personal story that ends well. There will always be unexpected plot twists and those who try to block our path to fulfillment and joy, yet we can rest assured that the eventual story of our life will be a triumph. The freedom to choose is a sacred gift we must never take for granted. Love is always the lesson and the reward.

- How do I learn to forgive?
- How do I become a better person after experiencing a destructive relationship?
- What brings me peace?
- What brings me joy?
- Who do I love?
- Who loves me?

- How do I learn to trust again?
- How do I view my abuser?
- What have I learned from my experience with neglect?
- How can I bless lives?
- How do I develop self-confidence and humility?
- What are my priorities?
- Do I really know what love is?
- How do I learn to trust after being betrayed?
- How do I let go of my fear?
- Have I held my abuser accountable for his behavior?
- Have I held myself accountable for my behavior?
- How do I move forward with my life?
- When do I know it is time to leave a destructive relationship?
- How do I tell the difference between indifference, disinterest, and neglect?
- How do I learn to love myself?
- Can the quality of my relationships be improved?
- Am I abusing or neglecting someone close to me?
- Am I allowing myself to be abused and neglected?
- What have I learned about relationships?
- Where do I go from here?
- Can my pain be transformed into love?

Notes

ABOUT *the* AUTHOR

Janene Baadsgaard has written extensively with warmth, valuable information, insight, and humor about family life for over thirty years. She is the author of hundreds of newspaper columns and features, many magazine articles, and over a dozen books. She is a graduate of Brigham Young University in communications with a journalism emphasis and has taught courses in writing and literature for Utah Valley State College (presently Utah Valley University). A popular speaker, Janene has shared her wit and wisdom with thousands at popular univesity events and conferences as well as at numerous other civic and church-sponsored events. She is the mother of ten children and grandmother to many. She lives on two acres in Spanish Fork, Utah. Her hobbies include reading, writing, singing, playing the piano and violin, and gardening.

Some of her books titles include *Is There Life After Birth?*, *A Sense of Wonder*, *Why Does My Mother's Day Potted Plant Always Die?*, *On the Roller-Coaster Called Motherhood*, *Families Who Laugh . . . Last*, *Grin and Share It: Raising a Family With a Sense of Humor*, *Sister Bishop's Christmas Miracle*, *Expecting Joy*, *Winter's Promise*, *Fifteen Secrets to a Happy Home*, *For Every Mother*, *Family Finances for the Flabbergasted*, and *Healing from Abuse*.